Lectionary Tales For The Pulpit

Series VI
Cycle A

David Leininger

CSS Publishing Company, Inc., Lima, Ohio

Copyright © 2007 by
CSS Publishing Company, Inc.
Lima, Ohio

Most scripture quotations are from the Holy Bible, New International Version. Copyright © 1973, 1978, 1984 International Bible Society. Used by permission of Zondervan Bible Publishers. All rights reserved.

Some scripture quotations are taken from the King James Version of the Bible, in the public domain.

Some scripture quotations are taken from The Message by Eugene H. Peterson, copyright © 1993, 1994, 1995, 1996, 2000, 2001, 2002. Used by permission of NavPress Publishing Group. All rights reserved.

For more information about CSS Publishing Company resources, visit our website at www.csspub.com or email us at custserv@csspub.com or call (800) 241-4056.

ISSN: pending

Cover design by Barbara Spencer
ISBN-13: 978-0-7880-2454-2
ISBN-10: 0-7880-2454-X

PRINTED IN USA

Dedicated to the memory
of the first preacher I ever knew,
my dad,
The Reverend Milton N. Leininger

Table Of Contents

Advent 1   11
Isaiah 2:1-5
Swords Into Plowshares

Advent 2   14
Isaiah 11:1-10
The Wondrous Gift

Advent 3   17
Isaiah 35:1-10
Streams In The Desert

Advent 4   20
Matthew 1:18-25
Joseph

Christmas Eve/Christmas Day   23
Titus 2:11-14
All I Want For Christmas

Christmas 1   25
Matthew 2:13-23
When Evil Seems To Win

Christmas 2   27
Ephesians 1:3-14
What's Right With The Church?

The Epiphany Of Our Lord   30
Ephesians 3:1-12
The Christian Family

The Baptism Of Our Lord/Epiphany 1/Ordinary Time 1   32
Matthew 3:13-17
The Power Of Water

Epiphany 2/Ordinary Time 2   34
John 1:29-42
The Quintessential Evangelist

Epiphany 3/Ordinary Time 3   37
Matthew 4:12-23
Fish Bait

Epiphany 4/Ordinary Time 4   39.
Micah 6:1-8
Real Religion

Epiphany 5/Ordinary Time 5   41
Isaiah 58:3-9a (9b-12)
The Problem Of Hunger

Epiphany 6/Ordinary Time 6   44
1 Corinthians 3:1-9
Planting And Watering

Epiphany 7/Ordinary Time 7   46
Leviticus 19:1-2, 9-18
Sunday Dinner

Epiphany 8/Ordinary Time 8   49
Matthew 6:24-34
Stuff

Epiphany 9/Ordinary Time 9   51
Matthew 7:21-29
Hearing And Doing

The Transfiguration Of Our Lord
(Last Sunday After Epiphany)   54
Matthew 17:1-9
What Boggles Your Mind?

Ash Wednesday   56
Matthew 6:1-6, 16-21
Lent

Lent 1   58
Matthew 4:1-11
Temptation

Lent 2   60

Genesis 12:1-4a
The Adventure Of Faith

Lent 3   63

John 4:5-42
Who Woulda Thunk It?

Lent 4   65

John 9:1-41
Telling The Story

Lent 5   67

Ezekiel 37:1-14
The Ideal Pastor

Passion/Palm Sunday   70

Philippians 2:5-11
A Drama In Three Acts

Maundy Thursday   72

John 13:1-17, 31b-35
The Upper Room

Good Friday   75

John 18:1—19:42
The Blame Game

Easter Day   78

John 20:1-18
Rolling Stones

Easter 2   80

1 Peter 1:3-9
God's Ultimate Cosmic Joke

Easter 3   83

Luke 24:13-35
East Of Easter

Easter 4   86

Psalm 23
The Shepherd Psalm

Easter 5   89

1 Peter 2:2-10
Christ Our Cornerstone

Easter 6   91
    Acts 17:22-31
    Attack Or Attract?

The Ascension Of Our Lord   94
    Acts 1:1-11
    Clouded Vision

Easter 7   97
    John 17:1-11
    Sounds Just Like Mom

The Day Of Pentecost   100
    Acts 2:1-21
    The Force

The Holy Trinity   102
    2 Corinthians 13:11-13
    Speaking Of God

Proper 4/Pentecost 2/Ordinary Time 9   105
    Genesis 6:9-22; 7:24; 8:14-19
    Under The Rainbow

Proper 5/Pentecost 3/Ordinary Time 10   108
    Romans 4:13-25
    God's Not Done With Me Yet!

Proper 6/Pentecost 4/Ordinary Time 11   112
    Matthew 9:35—10:8 (9-23)
    Uncommon Laborers

Proper 7/Pentecost 5/Ordinary Time 12   116
    Genesis 21:8-21
    How *Not* To Be The Father Of The Year

Proper 8/Pentecost 6/Ordinary Time 13   119
    Genesis 22:1-14
    The Second Worst Story In The Bible

Proper 9/Pentecost 7/Ordinary Time 14   122
    Matthew 11:16-19, 25-30
    Ask The Average Person

Proper 10/Pentecost 8/Ordinary Time 15   125
    Matthew 13:1-9, 18-23
    Fertility Facts

Proper 11/Pentecost 9/Ordinary Time 16   128
    Genesis 28:10-19a
    I Am With You

Proper 12/Pentecost 10/Ordinary Time 17   130
    Romans 8:26-39
    Nevertheless

Proper 13/Pentecost 11/Ordinary Time 18   133
    Matthew 14:13-21
    Bring Them To Me

Proper 14/Pentecost 12/Ordinary Time 19   135
    Matthew 14:22-33
    Little Faith

Proper 15/Pentecost 13/Ordinary Time 20   138
    Genesis 45:1-15
    Payback Time

Proper 16/Pentecost 14/Ordinary Time 21   141
    Matthew 16:13-20
    Who Do You Say That I Am?

Proper 17/Pentecost 15/Ordinary Time 22   144
    Exodus 3:1-15
    The Bush Is Still Burning

Proper 18/Pentecost 16/Ordinary Time 23   148
    Exodus 12:1-14
    Remembering 9/11

Proper 19/Pentecost 17/Ordinary Time 24   151
    Matthew 18:21-35
    The Power To Change The Past

Proper 20/Pentecost 18/Ordinary Time 25   154
    Philippians 1:21-30
    To Die Is Gain

Proper 21/Pentecost 19/Ordinary Time 26   157
    Philippians 2:1-13
    Salvation

Proper 22/Pentecost 20/Ordinary Time 27   160
    Exodus 20:1-4, 7-9, 12-20
    God Cares About Justice

Proper 23/Pentecost 21/Ordinary Time 28   163
    Philippians 4:1-9
    Church Fights

Proper 24/Pentecost 22/Ordinary Time 29   165
    Matthew 22:15-22
    One Nation, Under God

Proper 25/Pentecost 23/Ordinary Time 30   167
    Deuteronomy 34:1-12
    The God Of The Unlikely

Reformation Day   170
    John 8:31-36
    The Truth

All Saints   172
    1 John 3:1-3
    Family Resemblance

Proper 26/Pentecost 24/Ordinary Time 31   174
    Joshua 3:7-17
    Memorial Day

Proper 27/Pentecost 25/Ordinary Time 32   176
    1 Thessalonians 4:13-18
    Words Of Comfort

Proper 28/Pentecost 26/Ordinary Time 33   179
    Matthew 25:14-30
    Talents

Christ The King/Proper 29   181
    Matthew 25:31-46
    The Incredible Invitation

Thanksgiving Day   183
    Luke 17:11-19
    Leaping Lepers

Swords Into Plowshares

September 11th. There are not many dates on the calendar that, simply by mentioning them, makes the hair on our necks stand on end. This is one. December 7 is one, although less so now than in years past. September 11 will suffer the same fate over the course of time, but for this generation, September 11 is the "day that will live in infamy."

United States citizens were grateful to the world for its out-pouring of support — the sounds of "The Star-Spangled Banner" playing at Buckingham Palace, on the streets of Paris, and at Berlin's Brandenburg Gate; South Korean children gathering to pray out-side the US embassy in Seoul; prayers of sympathy offered at a mosque in Cairo. The nation will not forget moments of silence and days of mourning in Australia and Africa and Latin America, nor will America forget the citizens of eighty other nations who died with our own: dozens of Pakistanis; more than 130 Israelis; more than 250 citizens of India; men and women from El Salva-dor, Iran, Mexico, and Japan; and hundreds of British citizens.

To be honest, there has never been a time in our lives when the world has been so united. What occurred on September 11, 2001, mesmerized every nation on earth and presented an unprecedented opportunity to build upon international goodwill. With the whole world unified as never before in horror over the atrocities perpe-trated, a global commitment to avoid violence and war as a means of settling disputes or grievances was possible.

What kind of world would we have now if, instead of repaying evil with evil, the response could have been along the following lines. Noting that the people of Afghanistan had suffered greatly

11

under the oppressive Taliban regime, rather than threatening innocent Afghani citizens with attacks as undeserved as what befell men and women in the twin towers on September 11. What if a different response was proposed? The world was aware at the time that Afghanistan was in the grip of a three-year famine and the UN was estimating 5.5 million Afghans would soon be starving. Suppose America had begun sending aid to Afghanistan on a scale not seen since the Marshall plan. Against the will of the Taliban, suppose America poured food, medicine, and materials into the country. Our response to the Al Qaeda outrage would not be an act of revenge but an act of mercy. How sweet it would have been to see the people scrambling for American food in the dust created by their Taliban masters! How sweet to see in the eyes of those peasants, not the easy hatred inspired by war, but the uneasy question: "Can it really be the 'Great Satan' that feeds the starving?" If ever the Christian message — "Love your enemies and pray for those who persecute you" — had strategic relevance, it was here. How would our world be different now if this had been the response to 9/11 rather than the violence that ensued?

Such an approach has already been shown to work in the nation of South Africa. On an April day in 1994, they came by the tens of thousands. They formed lines that sometimes snaked for more than a mile. They waited patiently for two, five, even twelve hours. One handicapped woman came in a wheelbarrow pushed by relatives. Never allowed to vote before, black South Africans were voting for the first time in their lives. That signaled a major breakthrough in that nation. Political control was shifting from the white minority to the black majority who had endured years and years of oppression under Apartheid. Only a few years ago, many observers of South Africa were predicting that only a bloody revolution could overturn the brutal white-controlled government. But in a remarkable turn of events, a black leader imprisoned for 26 years and a white leader willing to change worked together for a new South Africa. The world has seen it — non-violent change *is* possible!

The call is for people of faith to commit to the kind of world in which all of us can live together, the kind of world envisioned by the ancient prophet Isaiah, a world where "They will beat their swords into plowshares and their spears into pruning hooks. Nation will not take up sword against nation, nor will they train for war anymore." A wonderful word of hope as we await the coming of the Prince of Peace.

The Wondrous Gift

Phillips Brooks was an eloquent Episcopalian preacher in the nineteenth century, famed in his day for his great oratory, his outspoken calls for the abolition of slavery, and his support of Abraham Lincoln. After the War Between the States, Brooks took a pilgrimage to the Holy Land and found himself in Bethlehem on Christmas Eve where, after visiting the Field of the Shepherds, he attended the midnight service in the Church of the Nativity. It was a moving and memorable experience for him, and on his return to America, he recorded his impressions in the form of a hymn for the children of his Sunday school. It was set to music by his church organist, Lewis Redner. You know the words:

> *O little town of Bethlehem,*
> *How still we see thee lie;*
> *Above thy deep and dreamless sleep,*
> *The silent stars go by.*

Beautiful words, beautiful music.

> *How silently, how silently,*
> *The wondrous Gift is giv'n;*
> *So God imparts to human hearts*
> *The blessings of His heav'n.*

"Wondrous gift" ... a good description of what happened that night in Bethlehem. The gracious gift of a loving God, to be sure.

14

For us who have heard the Christmas story over and over and over again, we are content to call the gift beautiful or marvelous or any number of other adjectives to reflect our happiness at God's goodness to us. But the dictionary defines "wondrous" as something "commanding wonder ... surprise." We have heard the story too many times to be surprised by it anymore, but put yourself in the position of the folks who first heard the tale. After all, for generations they had heard words like those from the prophet Isaiah that God would send a "shoot from the stump of Jesse," a Messiah, a Savior, a deliverer. And now God had done it. But the gift of that child is certainly not what anyone might have expected.

He was not born like a Messiah. Who could imagine such nonsense as a manger with animals and shepherds? To the people of old Israel, the least they might have expected would have been a birth in the home of the high priest surrounded by the most devout of the day. It would have been perfectly acceptable to have had the nativity in Caesar's palace surrounded by pomp and splendor. But among animals? Ridiculous.

As that baby grew, he neither *looked* nor *acted* like a Messiah. The people of old Judea were expecting someone to come along in a cloud of dust on a white horse with some ancient equivalent of "Hi-yo Silver!" They wanted a political and military leader who would free them from Rome. They wanted a mighty king.

Perhaps that is part of the magic of it all. God could have had the Messiah be born in Caesar's palace or in the home of the high priest. That baby could have grown into a powerful political figure who would lead his people to victory over the Legions of Rome. He could have died peacefully in bed at a ripe old age. What a tiresome story that would have been. But, after 2,000 years of telling, we never tire of hearing about the sheep and the manger and the star that shone over Bethlehem. We never tire of hearing of Jesus' humility and compassion. We never tire of hearing the story of his death and miraculous resurrection. God must get a great chuckle every year over this wonderful joke on humankind, we who are almost always impressed by outward appearances. The King of kings, cradled in a manger ... dying on a cross.

15

O holy child of Bethlehem,
Descend to us, we pray;
Cast out our sin and enter in;
Be born in us today.

Streams In The Desert

"... Gladness and joy will overtake them, and sorrow and sighing will flee away." Sure does sound like Christmas, doesn't it?

It would be wonderful if everyone could feel it. But the wars go on. Families that have lost loved ones are preparing for a holiday that they could have never imagined. There is a certain dissonance to the season. Trips to malls and stores with the sacred Muzak in the air singing of "Joy To The World" or "God Rest Ye Merry, Gentlemen" mock the harsh realities.

Do you remember television's *Ally McBeal*? One particular episode opened with Ally slowly making her way home after some Christmas shopping when she spies a man standing in a cemetery looking down through tears at a new gravestone. Ally gently asks if there is anything she can do. The response: not unless you are an angel ... or a prophet. As he turns to Ally, his overcoat, open at the neck, reveals a clerical collar; it turns out he is a Methodist minister. He tells Ally that the gravestone belongs to his wife, just recently murdered by a nervous robber who shot her while she fumbled too long in her purse. He also notes that he has just lost his job — his congregation's administrative board fired him. Why? "They say because I can no longer do my job."

"Why do they say you can no longer do your job?"

"Because I don't believe in God."[1]

Oh.

Far-fetched? A minister losing his faith? It can happen. And if it can happen there, it can happen anywhere. Ancient Israel would have been a candidate. The mighty empire of Babylon had conquered the tiny nation of Judah; all that remained of the great kingdom of David and Solomon. They had stripped that nation bare. Whole cities had been burned to the ground. They took the crops and livestock of every farmer and left nothing but scorched earth. They killed or captured the rulers, the teachers, the scientists, the priests, the heads of corporations, and took the survivors to Babylon as prisoners. The physical and emotional and spiritual devastation was horrible.

The book of Lamentations captures the desolation in its mournful poetry. "How deserted lies the city, once so full of people ... All her people groan as they search for bread; they barter their treasures for food to keep themselves alive ... They say to their mothers, 'Where is bread and wine?' as they faint like wounded men in the streets of the city, as their lives ebb away in their mothers' arms" (Lamentations 1 & 2 *passim*). Picture the destruction and poverty in Europe following World War II, or the images of children foraging for food. Or hear the weeping of people culling through the remains of their homes after the bombing of their city. It was to these sad people that Isaiah 35 came.

As they picked through the ruins of their lives, the prophet gave them a beautiful vision of the future. Farms had reverted to wild ground, but that land would be covered again with flowers and fruit. All the trees had been cut down either for warfare or for firewood. But soon the land would be covered with the cedars of Lebanon, trees so big it would take twelve people to encircle their trunks. In many places, rivers and springs had been poisoned, wells had been destroyed, dams and levees had been ruined. But once again, water would flow in the desert to replace the mirages on the sand. Villages had been abandoned, but were now the headquarters for thieves and scavengers. Soon they would again be safe places, filled with people, a time when "the eyes of the blind [will] be opened and the ears of the deaf unstopped. Then will the lame leap like a deer, and the mute tongue shout for joy." Wow!

Isaiah presents a wonderfully hope-filled scene. As these folks who long ago gave up looking for any joy in living, these who have suffered a period of spiritual or emotional "exile" because of a long illness, recovery from addiction, or even the tragic death of someone very special, whether in a television drama like *Ally McBeal*, the global-impact drama of wars and violence, or any of life's cruel and painful dramas in between, as these desperate people scavenge the ruins of their lives, they see an eruption. "The desert and the parched land will be glad; the wilderness will rejoice and blossom. Like the crocus, it will burst into bloom ... Water will gush forth in the wilderness and streams in the desert. The burning sand will become a pool, the thirsty ground bubbling springs." Life everywhere!

And in the midst of it, there is singing. The sound is distant at first. But it swells and grows. Then a mighty parade comes into view. The ransomed of the Lord — those who had languished in exile — return to their homeland. There will indeed be "Joy to the world, the Lord is come." Yes! "Gladness and joy," says the prophet, "and sorrow and sighing will flee away." And all God's people ... people then and people now and people forevermore ... *all* God's people can say, "Amen!" And Amen! And Amen again!

---

1. David E. Kelley, "Nine One One," *Ally McBeal*, FOX Broadcasting, 12/10/01.

Joseph

What a mess! Put yourself in Joseph's sandals. A simple man, a carpenter. He is about to be married. It would be the normal Jewish three-step procedure. There was the engagement, which was often made when the couple were only children, usually through the parents or a professional matchmaker. And it was often made without the couple involved ever having seen each other. Marriage was considered far too serious a step to be left to the dictates of the human heart. Then there was the betrothal, which was the ratification of the engagement into which the couple had previously entered. It lasted for one year during which the couple was known as man and wife, although they would not live together. Betrothal could only be terminated as a full-blown marriage could be — by death or divorce. The third stage was the marriage proper, which took place at the end of the year of betrothal.

Joseph and Mary were at stage two. Suddenly, Mary turns up pregnant. And the baby is not Joseph's. Joseph *knows* it is not his. What a nightmare!

What a jumble his feelings must have been! Rage? Unquestionably. Fury at her unfaithfulness. Fury at whomever had defiled the marriage bed with her. Embarrassment? Of course. Half his friends would think he was a fool for having been cuckolded, and the other half would think that he did not have enough self-control to wait until after the marriage feast. Sorrow? No doubt. His life was planned out — it was going to be with Mary. Now that would not be possible. Sorry for her, too, even though this was something she had brought on herself.

Now what? Jewish law allowed stoning as the penalty for adultery, but that was a sentence not often carried out in practice. Joseph could have made a public spectacle of Mary to prove his own innocence in the affair. No, finally, the decision was made to handle the situation quietly, to give her a Bill of Divorcement in the presence of two witnesses as the law required, and then let her go her way. Perhaps she would return to the home of her cousin Elizabeth to avoid the shame of having the child in Nazareth. One way or another, the nightmare would be over.

But we know the story does not end there. He was asleep, but sometime during the night, was awakened with a start. "Joseph. Joseph. Wake up."

"What?" He looked around in the dark of his room, the only light from the moon beaming through the window. He saw the silhouette of a man. But there was something about him that told Joseph there was no reason to fear.

The silhouette spoke. "Joseph, son of David, do not be afraid to take Mary as your wife, for the child conceived in her is from the Holy Spirit. She will bear a son, and you are to name him Jesus, for he will save his people from their sins."

Joseph had no chance to reply — the visitor disappeared. What would Joseph have said anyway? We can see him lying there thinking until morning, then, at daybreak, trying to figure out what had happened. Had there really been anyone there the night before? Perhaps it had been a dream. Just a continuation of the nightmare? No. The message was from the Lord. It was too strange to have come from anyone else.

We know the rest of the story. Joseph came through. The betrothal was resumed. There was that trip down to Bethlehem for the Roman census, not much fun for a very pregnant young lady. The baby came. Joseph named him — that was the prerogative of the father, and Joseph accepted this child as his own, "of the house and lineage of David," as the old King James has it. Good man.

Howard Chapman is a Presbyterian minister in Iowa. He tells of an exercise he has used with his confirmation classes. He begins by letting them know that scholars think that Mary was the same age as they were, about fourteen or so. He then shows them

21

Deuteronomy 22:23-24, where according to Jewish law Joseph could have brought charges against Mary, and if found guilty, she could have been put to death. He then divides up the class with all the boys on one side and all the girls on the other. The girls' assignment is to list all of Mary's options, while the boys are to list Joseph's.

This usually generates a lively discussion, especially once they realize they do not have to stick to nice, neat, happy-ending choices. With not much prompting, they generate quite a list. Mary could have ... had an abortion, claimed she was raped, committed suicide, run away, and so on. Joseph, on the other hand, could have ... brought her to trial, quietly sent her out of town, left town himself, eloped with her, made up a story, and the like.

In one particular class, when all of these options were listed on the chalkboard, Howard stood back. He asked, "What does all this tell you?"

The class was very quiet for a moment or two. Then John, the worst troublemaker in the bunch, said, "Wow! Look at all that could have gone wrong. God was really taking a risk."

Smart kid. Indeed, since the beginning of creation, God has been willing to risk. But note one thing: this very first story in the New Testament, this story about Joseph, this story about the nightmare his life had become, this story about the angel's midnight message, this story ... is really *God's* story. From the first story until the last, the essence is caught in something as simple as a name. Emmanuel. God is with us. Remember that the next time your own life has become a nightmare. Emmanuel. We are not alone. God is with us.

All I Want For Christmas

"All I want for Christmas is my two front teeth." Remember that? Life is certainly simpler when we are told what someone wants. What I want this Christmas is the gift of grace!

Grace. The theologians among us will hear that word and think, "Aha! Grace ... the unmerited favor of God." Good definition. And I surely need that. But the grace I am thinking of is down one level, a bit more mundane. I also need the grace, the unmerited favor, of friends and neighbors, and especially brothers and sisters in Christ.

Why grace? Because somehow, over the course of recent years, there appears to be an inexorable shrinkage of the pool of grace available in our world. It is getting meaner and meaner and meaner out there. Have you noticed? For goodness sake, even the mortgage companies and bankers offer a bit of "grace" when things get tight, but other than that, no one seems willing to cut anyone any slack. We are a society that wants *what* it wants, *when* it wants it, and the *way* it wants it. And heaven help anyone who would dare to disappoint us, even inadvertently. If someone fails to meet our expectations, they should be fired or sued. History may look on ours as a "civilized" society (although that could be open to question), but we have become a not very "civil" society. Where is the grace anymore?

It would be lovely to say that the answer to that is in the church. Yes, it *ought* to be, but the church is often more reflective of what society *is* instead of what it *should* be, so even churches can be pretty uncivil places.

The story of Christmas is, at its heart, a story of grace. The coming of Jesus Christ into our world 2,000 years ago is the affirmation of God's unmerited favor to us. Scripture is clear. In churches that follow the lectionary tonight, people are hearing not only the account of Christ's birth in Luke, chapter 2, but also a brief epistle lesson from Titus, chapter 2, where Paul writes, "For the grace of God has appeared ... Jesus ... bringing salvation to all ..." Grace — the essence of Christmas.

Someone has suggested that love is like the Bible's loaves and fishes — it works best when given away. It is the same with grace. Perhaps we will have a more grace-filled society if we in the church who have been the recipients of God's marvelous grace in Christ Jesus will take it upon ourselves to begin giving it away. I can promise it will make a difference in each of our lives.

When Evil Seems To Win

"Peace on earth." Ha! Even in the Christmas story, it doesn't last long. The last strains of "Silent Night, Holy Night" have hardly sounded when Matthew confronts us with the slaughter of innocent babies.

Scholars point out that there are no other records of such a massacre. Nothing else in the New Testament mentions it. While Josephus tells us that Herod ordered the execution of three of his sons (even Caesar in Rome is reported to have said it was safer to be Herod's pig than Herod's son); and at his burial, one member of every family was to be slain so that the nation might really mourn,[1] he says nothing about any massacre in Bethlehem. Of course, the plot of a king fearing for his power and seeking to kill any possible usurpers is not uncommon. There is the somewhat similar incident in Moses' life as well as stories in Greek and Roman mythologies and in the folklore of Egypt and Babylon. Estimates are that Bethlehem had a population of approximately 1,000 at this point so the number of under-two-year-old baby boys would have been relatively small. Regardless, the horrific story is a jolting reminder that, just because of the arrival of Jesus, all is not suddenly right with the world.

That is no shock to anyone who knows subsequent history. The list of outrages and man's inhumanity to man is extensive: the Crusades, the Inquisition, the Holocaust, the genocides, one war after another after another in an unending stream. Mary, Joseph, and the baby were just three refugees out of millions and millions. It does indeed appear at times that God is not on the throne. Evil is.

25

Yes, there are times when we wonder. There are evil people — the sociopaths, the mass murders, the vicious child and spouse abusers. There are evil moments when otherwise good people are drawn in — My Lai, Haditha. There are evil systems in which we all participate — people going without food and shelter in a nation of abundance, people not getting medical care because of no other reason than lack of money, and people caught in the midst of war. There are even evils born of sheer stupidity. The novelist William Burroughs, during a drunken party in Mexico one night in 1951, undertook to play William Tell — he used a pistol to shoot a glass off his wife's head. He missed ... and put a bullet in her brain instead. How stupid. How evil. Yes, it often seems that the evil wins.

But the message of our faith says that evil does not have the last word. Herod does not win. Herod dies, and Jesus, Mary, and Joseph return from exile in Egypt. *Evil does not win!* With joy we can shout out that God's world does not end with either the whimper of a starving child or the blast of a nuclear bomb; it ends with the Lamb upon the throne and the victorious song of a massive choir singing words we have come to love: "The kingdoms of this world shall become the kingdoms of our Lord and of his Christ, And he shall reign forever and ever." Hallelujah!

---

1. Flavius Josephus, *Antiquities Of The Jews*, Book XVII , written between 66-74AD. p. 181. Can be found at http//www.earlyjewishwritings.com/josephus.html.

What's Right With The Church?

A denominational executive was scheduled to conduct an officers' retreat for a local church. The officers had several requests for topics to be covered during the sessions, one of which was some time spent talking about what is *right* with the church.

Strange questions for church officers — or perhaps not so strange. Perhaps these folks have fallen prey to the same beast that sometimes attacks us all ... the beast of familiarity, and as everyone knows "familiarity breeds contempt."

What about these officers? No doubt they have heard from unchurched friends that the church is nothing but a bunch of hypocrites. They have heard the theological controversies that seem to continually plague us. They have probably been to church committee and board meetings and have seen their brothers and sisters in Christ behave in most un-Christlike ways and wondered whether the church has really made any difference in people's lives. They know what is wrong with the church, but somewhere, down in the middle of the mess, they realize that that is not the whole story.

What is right with the church? Despite all we hear there must be something. After all, almost two billion people around the world are associated with it. Think about it for a moment. The church has done and continues to do a great deal that is right!

The church has given the world ideals: religious and political liberty, racial unity, social justice, and human brotherhood. Through the work of the church and the convictions, which have come from her, the most sinful of the world's economic and social and political evils have been driven to defeat or shamed into hiding. Who led the battle against human slavery in this nation in the nineteenth century? Who has been in the forefront of America's quest for racial equality? Who has been most vocal in its concern for peace among nations? The church and her people have been the conscience of the world.

The church has provided bold messengers, the first pioneers and adventurers into the dark and neglected areas of the earth — the William Careys, the David Brainards, the Hudson Taylors, the David Livingstons — not simply for the sake of pushing beyond frontiers but that the people who live there might come to know the fullness of God's blessing in Jesus Christ.

The messengers of the church, not medical people as such, have been the first to go into all parts of the earth with the science of sanitation, nutrition, and physical healing. How many hospitals are named "Baptist" or "Methodist" or "Presbyterian"?

Not professional educators but the messengers of the church have reduced languages to writing, established schools, and set up printing presses for the distribution of the Word of God. The first Sunday schools were established, not simply to teach Bible stories to youngsters, but to offer what was then the only opportunity for them to learn to read and write. Public education in America grew out of the selfless work of the church.

Not social reformers but the messengers of the church have taken the lead in the fight against poverty, famine, and plague. The church has elevated the status of women, created new conditions for childhood, established orphanages, day care centers, homes for the aged, and others who need help.

History offers no parallel to the unselfish and uplifting work of the church. There is no question that what goes on in legislative chambers, in council halls, and in the highest courts of the nations is always of importance to humanity. But when the world is out of joint, when people's minds are disoriented and their hearts are about to fail them for fear, thank God we have the church. With all of her sanctuaries of worship and her opportunities for service, where men and women come to have their faith strengthened, their conscience convicted, their convictions born, and their characters created. The church, for all her faults, is the institution that has made the most positive impact on the world through the ages.

But for all the good works the church has offered through history, those pale by comparison to the one thing that the church uniquely did and continues to do — it has introduced the world to Jesus Christ. With the writer to the Ephesians the church has proclaimed, "In him we have redemption through his blood, the forgiveness of sins, in accordance with the riches of God's grace."

The Christian Family

George Burns once quipped, "Happiness is having a large, loving, caring, close-knit family ... in another city." We know what he means.

The family has changed a great deal. The old *Ozzie & Harriet* model of Dad going off to work, Mom staying home and waiting for the children to return from school is now just a black-and-white piece of nostalgia — only a tiny percentage of America's families fit that picture; most do not. An elderly doctor listened to a woman complain about the disappearance of the old-fashioned family doctor. Finally, he lost patience and replied, "Madam, if you will show me an old-fashioned family, I will produce a doctor for it."

The American family these days could surely use a doctor, or someone to provide some healing. Years ago, the great English preacher of the past generation, Leslie Weatherhead, delivered a message called "What is God's Plan for the Family," in which he lamented a report from the Marriage Guidance Council in June 1945, reporting that 10% of marriages were finishing in the divorce court and that the figure would be 20% if separations were included. Talk about the "good old days." How about almost one-half of the marriages ending in divorce these days? Some 25% of Anglo children, 35% of Latino children, and 60% of African-American children are being raised by single parents. The modern family does need help.

People do not even agree on what constitutes a family anymore. Some time ago, a national insurance company requested that

1,200 randomly selected adults define the word "family." Surprisingly, only a small number, 22%, opted for the traditional definition: "a group of people related by blood, marriage, or adoption." A much larger percentage, nearly 75%, chose a much broader definition: "a group of people who love and care for each other."

To be sure, our "Christian Family" has nothing to do with blood or marriage. The "Christian Family" is one in which the members are related to Christ; the Christian Family is the church.

Ephesians makes that clear. In the early days of the faith, there was a serious problem concerning the understanding of who "qualified" to be a part of God's family. The issue then was both blood and marriage — racism — Jew versus Gentile. As bad as racial division has been and remains in modern society, it was even worse back then. The epistle writer realized the disastrous consequences of such an attitude, so he wrote to clear up any misunderstanding.

The estrangement Gentiles had previously experienced was noted. After all, a good Jew believed that the Gentiles were created by God to be fuel for the fires of hell; that God loved only Israel of all the nations that had been made. It was not lawful for a Jew to render help to a Gentile woman in childbirth for that would be to help bring another Gentile into the world; if a Jew married a Gentile, the *funeral* of that Jew was carried out. Even to go into a Gentile house rendered a Jew unclean.

The writer also knew the absolute segregation between Jew and Gentile in worship; he knew "the dividing wall," as he called it, the barrier in the temple court, beyond which no Gentile was permitted upon pain of death. In fact, Paul himself was finally imprisoned and killed after being wrongly accused of bringing the Gentile Trophimus beyond the barrier (Acts 21:28-29). But this good Jew was able to see beyond his tradition and write to the Gentile Christians in Ephesus, "through the gospel the Gentiles are heirs together with Israel, members together of one body, and sharers together in the promise in Christ Jesus." Family!

The Baptism Of Our Lord
Epiphany 1
Ordinary Time 1
Matthew 3:13-17

The Power Of Water

There is something powerful about water. The world saw it several years ago with the Christmas tsunami in south Asia. In America we have seen it in the aftermath of devastating hurricanes. Who could have imagined that water could be so powerful?

Truth be told, that is a trick question because the Christian church has always known it. This Sunday of the liturgical year is the day we remember the Baptism of the Lord. The scene down by the river. A throng of people from all walks of life. They have made a mini-pilgrimage into the countryside, come to see an itinerant preacher who is more than passing stranger: a coarse camel's hair tunic with a leather belt around his waist, the uniform of a prophet since the days of Elijah. They had come because there was a sense that something was missing in their walk with God, so they were ready to listen to a new voice. And this was a powerful voice.

Then one day it happened ... Jesus. The request for baptism. John's initial reluctance, then acquiescence. Finally, the dramatic climax. As Matthew records it, "As soon as Jesus was baptized, he went up out of the water. At that moment heaven was opened, and he saw the Spirit of God descending like a dove and lighting on him. And a voice from heaven said, 'This is my Son, whom I love; with him I am well pleased.' "

This changed everything! Jesus' baptism ushered in a new baptism. Christian baptism became not just a washing away of sin, as John's baptism was, but the baptism that brings the power of the Holy Spirit and a special relationship with God. Why? For no reason other than God chooses to do it.

Part of the message of Jesus' baptism and our own is that we are loved. Most folks understand that, and that is why they get all warm and fuzzy when it comes to presenting their little ones for the sacrament. But there is more: We have work to do. Remember, this happened at the *start* of Jesus' work. This was his commissioning service. Now, almost twenty centuries later, when someone is baptized in the church, whether infants or adults, it is no different. We still have work. We are receiving our commission.

If that is a bit scary, there is one more piece of good news about your baptism. Remember that picture at the Jordan — there is the crowd, John, Jesus, and the dove. The Holy Spirit. Do not forget the dove. Clearly, Matthew wants us to understand that from this moment on, Jesus and his ministry are empowered by the living presence of the Holy Spirit.

One Christmas Eve, our congregation witnessed the baptism of young Mitchell. Mitch was not as young as many of the children I baptize — he was almost ten years old. At the conclusion of the ceremony, I told him that this would be a day he would always remember, and that he and his pastor would have one special memory in common because it was on Christmas Eve, sixty years before, that I was baptized. My emotions welled up as I told him that and the words almost choked on the way out, something that happens to me regularly when I perform a baptism. Not because of some warm-fuzzy-isn't-this-a-nice-family picture kind of feeling, but because this is when the church gets dangerous. This sets someone on a journey that has the potential to change the world. And maybe because it is so dangerous, so threatening, so radical, that people either flee the church as they get older, or they weep when they have the opportunity to reaffirm their baptismal vows.

Who knew that water could be so powerful? Trick question. The church has always known.

The Quintessential Evangelist

With the decline of the mainline church, numerically, financially, and influentially, evangelism has become a continuing concern. Certainly, the church has always said evangelism is important, but our action (or lack of action) speaks even louder. One stuffy Presbyterian once called Dwight L. Moody to task for relying so much on emotion to win converts during his revivals. Moody's response? He admitted that his methods were not perfect, but he concluded, "I like my way of doing it better than your way of *not* doing it."

Some reluctance might be understandable because, for many, what passes for "evangelism" is something with which we want nothing to do. In my files, I have an old story the national news picked up that came out of the little town of Marion, North Carolina. Young Duffey Strode had been sent home from his first day at school, suspended for ten days. His crime? Preaching hellfire and damnation to his fellow students on the playground of the Eastfield Elementary School. The controversy was a continuation of one that had begun the year before. Duffey had staked out the back entrance to the school shouting out Bible verses condemning the other youngsters as whoremongers, adulterers, and fornicators, all with the purpose of calling them to repentance and winning them to Christ.

Frankly, when I was in elementary school, if someone had called me a whoremonger or a fornicator or an adulterer, I would not have had the foggiest notion what he meant. The only passions I had were baseball and peanut butter. I did not learn about the birds and the bees until I was twelve, and even then I was not sure I believed it. At any rate, I doubt that too many elementary school students would feel moved to repent of their whoremongering.

Duffey Strode was eleven years old when all this broke. Yes, children are more advanced these days than I was at the same age, but I doubt that he knew a great deal more about sexual sin than I did. Obviously, he had been spoon-fed those verses by his father, an unemployed machinist and self-styled street preacher himself. In a way, Mr. Strode can be applauded for being so sincere in his faith and bringing his children up the same way. We could applaud the sincerity with which people are called to repentance. We certainly applaud the sincerity with which he approached a task that too many Christians run from ... evangelism. Yes, the Strodes were nothing if not sincere. But most of us would probably add, sincerely wrong! That method of preaching the gospel will not effectively win anyone to Christ or the church.

Then what will win them? After all, the last thing the Lord told us to do, the Great Commission, was get out there and make disciples. It was not a suggestion. It was command!

Consider one fellow's efforts. This man was not well educated and his manner was somewhat rough and crude. He became a Christian and took the Lord's requirement seriously. He kept pestering his pastor to put him to work. Finally, the minister handed him a list of ten names with this explanation: "These are all members of the church, but they seldom attend. Some of them are prominent people in the community. Contact them about being more faithful. Here is some church stationery to write letters. Get them back in church."

The man accepted the challenge with rugged determination and enthusiasm. About three weeks later, a letter from a prominent physician whose name had been on the list arrived at the church office. Inside was a large check and a brief note: "Dear Pastor, enclosed is my check for $1,000 to help make up for my missing church so much, but be assured that I will be present this Lord's Day and each Lord's Day following. I will not by choice miss services again. Sincerely ... P.S. Would you please tell your secretary that there is only one 'T' in dirty and no 'C' in Skunk?"

Another "questionable" approach. The problem is that most Christians, especially those of us from relatively conservative mainline traditions, take no approach at all. Evangelism is the "E" word; there is something mildly disreputable about it. We feel uncomfortable about the images it conjures up: accosting people on the street and stuffing a tract in their hands; threatening people with the fires of eternal hell like young Duffey Strode unless they make a commitment; revival preachers interminably imploring "just one more" to raise that hand and make a decision for Christ; folks with bad hair on cable television begging folks to send more money to keep this soul-winning ministry on the air. That is not us. That is not our way of reaching people.

Do you know whose way *I* like? The fellow we meet in chapter 1 of John's gospel, Andrew, the apostle with the missionary heart. Apparently, he had always been a religious man — up until now he had been a disciple of John the Baptist, another fire and brimstone preacher in the manner of the Strodes. But one day Andrew met Jesus and Andrew was never the same again. Three times we find him on center stage in the gospel record: John 1, when he introduced his brother Simon to Christ; in John 6, when he introduced the boy with the loaves and fishes to Jesus; and in John 12, as he introduced some devout Greeks to the Savior. Andrew was always introducing people to the Lord. We do not know very much about Andrew other than that, but what we do know is wonderfully attractive ... and at the same time, a wonderful model for Christians who desperately need some help in doing "the 'E' word."

Fish Bait

A man was stopped by a game warden in a state park leaving a lake well known for its fishing, with two buckets of fish. The game warden asked, "Do you have a license to catch those fish?"

The man replied to the game warden, "No, sir. These are my pet fish."

"Pet fish?" the warden replied.

"Yes, sir. Every night I bring these here fish down to the lake and let them swim around for a while. I whistle and they jump back into their buckets, and I take 'em home."

"That's a bunch of hooey! Fish can't do that!"

The man looked at the game warden for a moment, and then said, "Here, I'll show you. It really works."

"Okay. I've *got* to see this!" The game warden was curious.

The man poured the fish into the river and stood and waited. After several minutes, the game warden turned to the man and said, "Well?"

"Well, what?" the man responded.

"When are you going to call them back?" the game warden prompted.

"Call who back?" the man asked.

"The fish!"

"What fish?" the man asked.

One more. The Reverend Dr. McStuffedshirt encountered one of his less-than-faithful parishioners returning from a day's fishing and engaged him in conversation. "Ah, Brother Jones," he began in

37

his best preaching tone, "you are a fine fisherman, but I am a fisher of men."

Jones, determined to get home after a long day, replied, "So I have heard. But I was passing your church last Sunday, and I looked in the window, and noticed you had not caught many...."

Today's gospel lesson is the source of that "fisher of men" designation. Unfortunately, as Paul Harvey has ruefully noted, these days "Too many Christians are no longer fishers of men but keepers of the aquarium."

There are several ways to interpret that phrase, "fishers of men." We could think of ourselves as the ones casting the nets — we spread the word far and wide in hopes that we will bring in a catch. Or we could think of ourselves as the net — we are the instrument the Lord uses to gather them in. But perhaps it might even be better if we would think of ourselves in terms of bait — fish bait. Unless they are born into the fellowship, that is, after all, the way new disciples are brought into the life of the church. Something attracts them, and most often it is you and me. Eighty percent of the people who join churches say they do it because someone — a friend or a relative — invited them. For good or ill, we are bait.

Real Religion

*He has told you, O mortal, what is good; and what does
the Lord require of you but to do justice, and to love
kindness, and to walk humbly with your God?*
— Micah 6:8

Familiar words. Perhaps you memorized them in Sunday school in years past, or perhaps you saw them inscribed on the wall of the Library of Congress. They are an ancient answer to the modern acronym that Christian youngsters wear on T-shirts, bracelets, and necklaces: WWJD — What Would Jesus Do? These few words spell it out. What is real religion? In other words, WWJHMD — What Would Jesus Have *Me* Do? After all, real religion is an attempt to answer that as well as the prophet's question, "What does the Lord require of you?" Here we have it in a nutshell, and it is as valid today as it was 2,800 years ago. Do justice, love kindness, walk humbly with your God.

It was in the latter part of the eighth century BC that Micah prophesied. He was a young contemporary of Isaiah, Hosea, and Amos. He and Isaiah brought God's message to the people of Judah in the south while Hosea and Amos took it north to Israel. It was a period of turmoil and change. Assyria was fast becoming a world power to challenge the hegemony of Egypt. There was one battle after another with the little nations used only as pawns in the wider struggle. Israel and Judah were constantly threatened by one power or another. It was a difficult time.

Like Amos, Micah was a product of the countryside, a farmer; like farmers throughout the centuries, he had a certain mistrust of city slickers. In his case, he had good reason: It was the city slickers who were fleecing the folks of the countryside that Micah knew as friends and neighbors; it was city slicker judges who took bribes to render unfair judgments; city slicker priests who were immoral and corrupt; city slicker prophets who would prophesy anything you might want in exchange for a few shekels. No wonder Micah thought of the cities as cesspools of sin.

To be sure, he had plenty to complain about concerning the nation's religious habits. It was bad enough that the prophets and priests were not living up to expectations, but the reason they were not was that the people did not want them to. The only preaching they wanted to hear was "God's in his heaven and all's right with the world." Micah even joked about it: "If a liar and deceiver comes and says 'I will prophesy for you plenty of wine and beer,' he would be just the preacher for this people" (2:11). They did not want to be embarrassed by anyone who would have called them to account for their behavior.

It was time for them to hear a word from the Lord. Micah came to them with a message that was not only valid for his own age, but for every age to come.

Do justice — love kindness — a humble walk with God. Sounds very much like the answer to WWJD — What Would Jesus Do? In fact, it is in Jesus that we see what justice and loving-kindness look like in a walk with God. WWJD. Jesus is still looking for followers. Not admirers, followers. So the correct question for you and me is "WWJHMD? What Would Jesus Have *Me* Do?"

The Problem Of Hunger

The problem of hunger in the world never seems to go away. Those who keep track of these things say more than 850 million people across the world are hungry, a number that is on the increase. Every day, more than 16,000 children die from hunger-related causes — one child every five seconds. Most poor people who battle hunger deal with chronic undernourishment and vitamin or mineral deficiencies, which result in stunted growth, weakness, and heightened susceptibility to illness. According to the World Health Organization, poor nutrition and calorie deficiencies cause nearly one in three people to die prematurely or have disabilities.

Even more amazing (or frightening), here in America, the richest nation in the history of the world, we still have a problem with hunger. Based on a US Census Bureau survey, in 2000, 10.5 million US households were "food insecure," meaning that they did not have access to enough food to meet their basic needs. About 33 million people lived in these households, including 20 million adults and 13 million children. Hunger in America has been, and continues to be, a real problem for a significant part of our population. Approximately 7 million different people receive assistance in any given week. One household in ten in this nation experiences hunger or the risk of hunger.

Another fact, this one not so sad, is that we do have enough food in the world. World production of grain alone is over 1.5 billion tons, enough to supply the entire world population with two pounds a day. This, with the current production of vegetables, fruits, nuts, and meat, is enough to supply each man, woman, and child with 3,000 calories a day — equal to the consumption of the average American. There is enough food: The problem is that some people cannot afford to pay the price of the available food. World hunger and malnutrition is a matter of poverty and accessibility, not production.

A participant at an anti-hunger conference told of a staff member from a food share program who tried to explain the problem of hunger to an elementary school class, and who got a lesson in it himself. To introduce the issue, the man asked the children how many of them had eaten breakfast that morning. As he expected, only a few raised their hands. So he continued, "How many of you skipped breakfast this morning because you don't like breakfast?" Lots of hands went up. "And how many of you skipped breakfast because you did not have time for it?" Many other hands went up.

He was pretty sure by then why the remaining children had not eaten, but he did not want to ask them about poverty, so he asked, "How many of you skipped breakfast because your family does not usually eat breakfast?" A few more hands were raised. Then he noticed a small boy whose hand had not gone up at all. Thinking the boy had not understood, he asked, "Why didn't you eat breakfast this morning?" The boy replied, his face serious, "It wasn't my turn."

For God's people, ending hunger is not simply a task to be undertaken as civilized human beings. Rather, it is the clear and unmistakable demand of our Lord. Yes, it is morally wrong, it is a *sin*, to allow millions of children and adults in America, plus countless millions more around the world, to suffer hunger when we *can* do something about it.

In the Old Testament, the prophets were crystal clear in their denunciation of people who claimed to be religious but did nothing to feed hungry neighbors. Listen again to Isaiah as he speaks for God and describes the kind of religious practice that is truly acceptable: "Is not this the kind of fasting I have chosen: to loose the chains of injustice and untie the cords of the yoke, to set the oppressed free and break every yoke? Is it not to share your food with the hungry and to provide the poor wanderer with shelter —

when you see the naked, to clothe him, and not to turn away from your own flesh and blood? ... if you spend yourselves in behalf of the hungry and satisfy the needs of the oppressed, then your light will rise in the darkness, and your night will become like the noonday."

Epiphany 6
Ordinary Time 6
1 Corinthians 3:1-9

Planting And Watering

I am a Presbyterian Christian, and I am proud of my heritage. Presbyterians trace our roots to John Calvin in Geneva, John Knox in Scotland, and here in America, to an Irish missionary by the name of Francis Makemie who came to preach in the colonies at the beginning of the eighteenth century. The first presbytery (the regional body which encompasses Presbyterian churches in a certain geographical area) in the new world was formed in Philadelphia in 1707. The first national organization of Presbyterians 1789.

It was May 21 of that year, to be exact, a rainy Thursday. An old man, hair all gray and figure showing too much enjoyment of good food, clumped his way slowly into the pulpit. The sight in his right eye was all but gone, lost in a voyage to England five years before. But John Witherspoon was not to be denied. Thirteen years earlier, and two blocks down the street, he had affixed his signature to a Declaration of Independence, which announced the freedom of his adopted country from the nation of his birth. Now he was participating in a putting-together rather than a declaring-apart, and this one last time his friends had chosen him to preside. Scotch accent repressed as usual in his public speaking, he called the commissioners to order — thirty or so men representing just under a dozen presbyteries. The first General Assembly of the Presbyterian Church in the United States of America was in session.

Witherspoon's one good eye was not that good, but no matter; he had been committing his sermons to memory for years, and this was a scripture he had used before. He preached to them from 1 Corinthians 3:7 — in the lilting language of the King James Bible,

44

"So then neither is he that planteth anything, neither he that watereth; but God that giveth the increase."

That was a word needed by those men. This first general assembly had been called in response to the continuing growth of Presbyterian witness on these shores. New churches had been established, then connected with one another in presbyteries and synods. It would have been easy for the commissioners to fly off to heights of inordinate pride in the accomplishments of the American Presbyterians, but Dr. Witherspoon's word about who is responsible for growth brought them back to earth.

I wonder what he might say to American Presbyterians today? Or, for that matter, what would a John Wesley say to Methodists or Henry Muhlenburg to Lutherans or Samuel Seabury to Episcopalians in light of the decline of the mainline church in numbers and influence since those heady days of expansion? Why the losses? Has God stopped giving increases? Or perhaps have we cut back on planting and watering?

This is no trivial matter. We are in an era of swift and stunning social change — continuing moral confusion; an ongoing mistrust of institutions; a government that often seems out of touch. If the mainline church, the church that provided the moral compass for this nation during our first 200 years, continues to decline, who will shape our nation's values as we move farther into the twenty-first century? Will it be those who are the heirs of Witherspoon, Wesley, Muhlenburg, and Seabury? Or are we willing to take our chances with whatever or whomever comes along? For those of us who *care* about the future, that is too big a gamble.

Sunday Dinner

How many folks have tried to read the Bible all the way through but never were able to finish? A staggering number, probably. They did fine getting through Genesis and the great stories of Abraham, Isaac, Jacob, and Joseph. Exodus was not bad, especially the first half with the stories of Moses and the escape from slavery in Egypt. But the book of Leviticus proved to be a bit much — all those ancient rules and regulations, instructions for priests, directions for sacrifices, dietary laws, and so on got to be like wading in molasses. Finally, the high resolve of reading the whole Bible through was abandoned as an impossible job.

No question, a good bit of Leviticus does not have much to say to modern Christians (which is the reason there is so little preaching from that book as well as the fact that this Sunday is the only one all year that calls for a Leviticus lection). But there is an extended portion, chapters 17-26, known as the Holiness Code — divine rules for living as a uniquely godly community — that contains some of the loftiest ethical teaching in all of scripture. There are commands to honor our parents and the elderly, to be honest in business dealings, and to be sensitive to the physically handicapped. It is the original source of Jesus' commandment to "Love your neighbor as yourself." It is worth our attention.

In the midst of these ethical instructions, we find one of those passages that seems not to apply anymore (which may be why the lectionary committee skipped them), those verses saying that when one brings an animal offering to the temple, all the meat has to be eaten the same day or the next day and that it would be a very serious infraction to eat any of it on the third day (19:5-8). The usual interpretation of the rule is that in a hot climate like the Middle East, meat spoiled rapidly without refrigeration (which did not exist then) and would be unhealthy to eat 48 hours after cooking. But there are two problems with that. First, do you really have to pass a law, especially such a strongly worded law, telling folks not to eat spoiled food? I suspect you could depend on people to figure that out for themselves. And second, what would such a health regulation be doing in a chapter of ethical instruction?

Let me offer another interpretation. If a man brought an animal offering to the temple, an offering in celebration of some happy event, and knew that it had to be totally consumed in two days, what would he do? Rather than waste the meat (which was a relatively precious commodity in an agricultural society), he would invite more of his relatives and neighbors. He would share some of it with the poor, the beggars waiting on the temple grounds hoping for such an invitation. By setting the regulation in the midst of ethical instruction, God's message appears to be that there is something actually ethical, something right, about the simple act of eating with one another.

Down deep, I think we know that. A shared meal binds people together. Any child can tell you that when you share your candy bar with the new child down the street, it is an act that produces instant friendship (just as two teenagers on a date sipping the same ice cream soda through two straws know that a special bond has been formed). Remember the movie, *Guess Who's Coming to Dinner*, and the furor caused by the daughter inviting the "wrong" sort of fellow for a meal? Eating together means something more than collectively fending off hunger. It helps us understand why ancient Israel was taught to bring the sacrifice and share it — it was a way of making the participants feel that they were linked to each other.

Sadly, there are not many opportunities to do that anymore. The pace of modern life has seen to that. We eat many of our meals with strangers, in cafeterias and restaurants, even jammed together on airplanes. Mealtime becomes like a ride in an elevator — there are other people around but we are expected to pretend not to be aware of them. Families no longer eat together like they used to,

47

and when they do, there is seldom a sense of an important shared experience. Eating has become a mundane matter of refueling our bodies the way we gas up our cars. And that is too bad. We have taken one more thing, which used to be rich in meaning and made it ordinary. No wonder there is so little magic left in our lives.

I wish we could get back to that big deal known as Sunday dinner that we experienced in years past. One of our favorite memories of a former congregation was Sunday dinner with the Robinsons. The Robinsons are a huge family that gathers every Sunday at Mama's — it is an army of brothers, sisters, husbands, wives, and cousins tearing around and screaming like banshees, hearing mothers and fathers yelling at them to watch out for their Sunday clothes and each other's skulls. Every so often, the preacher and his family would be invited to join them. Of course, as the resident "Holy Man" I was the designated pray-er ... careful not to go on too long with the blessing. It was wonderful. No one will ever have to explain to any of the Robinson clan what it means to be family; no one will ever have to explain what it means to belong or be loved — Sunday dinner takes care of that.

In a way, that is what we do as we gather at the Lord's table. The bit of bread and sip of juice will not do much to fend off physical hunger; but the hunger we all feel, the hunger for connectedness, for community, for family, for assurance that we are not alone in this world is surely fed. How does it happen? No one can explain it. As John Calvin said, "I should rather experience it than understand it."

Stuff

Jesus' words about "stuff" hit us right where we live. If there is any idolatry that is rampant in American society, it is this idolatry of "stuff."

If it is any consolation, the problem is not new. The people who heard Jesus on that Judean hillside had the same problem. Jesus said not to worry about "stuff" — God knows what you need and will provide for you just as the birds of the air are fed and the lilies of the field are dressed. And if God will take care of the birds and flowers so well, think how well *you* will be taken care of.

Jesus went on, "What it boils down to is this: If you are going to be concerned about anything, it should be to see that the things that are important to God are equally important to you. Then you can be absolutely confident that everything else that you need will be taken care of." Or as the King James Version has it, "Seek ye first the kingdom of God and his righteousness, and all these things shall be added unto you."

I knew a man whose whole life was firmly grounded upon that promise. He was a minister. He never had much money, but he was absolutely faithful in his tithe, and in fact, generally gave a good deal more as God prospered him because he understood the tithe was a floor, not a ceiling. There were not many luxuries in his home, but there was never any lack of necessities. None of his six children missed out on going to college because there was not enough money. He never worried. His attitude was, "God has always provided enough so far; I know he always will."

After his death, the congregation he had served so long wanted to do something in his memory. They commissioned a bronze plaque to be cast and placed on the wall of the sanctuary where he had preached for so many years. At the bottom of that plaque was the verse that had meant so much to him throughout his life and ministry: "Seek ye first the kingdom of God and his righteousness, and all these things shall be added unto you." I had the privilege of preaching at the dedication service for that plaque. God had been faithful to that man. I know. He is the man to whom this book is dedicated. He was my father.

What is truly important? Not "stuff." "Stuff" can be gone in a flash ... or a flash flood. Jesus says, "Seek first the kingdom of God and his righteousness," or in a more modern rendering, "Make God's priorities *your* priorities," then everything else will fall into place. That is what is truly important.

Hearing And Doing

Construction advice was given us from a well-known carpenter. This story comes right at the end of Jesus' Sermon on the Mount. Two builders put up fine homes, but one built on a very shaky foundation — sand — while the other built on solid rock. When the rains came and the wind blew and the flood waters roared, the house built on sand was demolished while the house built on the rock remained unscathed. Makes sense. The Lord tells us very plainly what the meaning is: It is all about hearing and doing.

Consider what has led Jesus up to this point ... what has gone before in the sermon. Let me give you a whirlwind overview of these three remarkable chapters. He began with the Beatitudes, those attitudes that, not ought to be, but *will be*, for those who have turned their lives over to God's control. They will be "poor in spirit" — not proud of their own accomplishments, their own righteousness, because they know that there is nothing they have in which to take pride in the first place. They will "mourn" because of their failure to measure up to God's standard. They will be "meek" enough to accept God's instruction. They will "hunger and thirst after righteousness" because they will know there is no finer way to live. They will be merciful, pure in heart, peacemakers, and even willing to rejoice in enduring persecution for the sake of the Lord and the kingdom. To be sure, such a lifestyle is foreign to those outside of Christ and it is impossible for even those who are *in* Christ without his presence in our lives. But Jesus makes plain that these are the attitudes that will be for those who are the children of God.

51

Then he deals with ethics in the kingdom ... getting along with one another, being careful in our sexual relationships, being honest, handling insults, even loving our enemies. He talks about our relationship with God — making our religion more than just a big show, generous use of our possessions, genuine trust of our heavenly Father's provision for us. Finally, he discusses the danger of self-deception: deceiving ourselves about our own righteousness by being judgmental, making comparisons with others, deceiving ourselves about God's care, deceiving ourselves about the difficulty of the Christian life, and deceiving ourselves by giving credence to those he calls "false prophets."

The Sermon on the Mount is the Lord's paradigm for kingdom living. It encompasses virtually every phase of life. And now, here at the conclusion, he makes the point that just listening to the instruction is worthless. It *has* to be put into action!

We know that is true. If we go to a doctor to get healing for a sick body and we are told that we need to take some certain medicine, get a certain amount of rest, and then we fail to take the advice, we will not get well. If we go to an attorney and ask for help with a legal problem and find there are certain procedures to be followed and we choose *not* to follow them, the problem will not be solved. If we travel in a strange town and stop to get directions to our destination, if we choose not to follow those directions, we will get lost. Simply hearing what we should do, whether it be from a doctor or a lawyer or a gas station attendant, does us no good unless we are willing to put the instruction into action.

Someone has pointed out that the New Testament does not contain any book titled "The Plans and Objectives of the Apostles." Rather we find the "*Acts* of the Apostles." Success comes from action, not simply thinking or reflecting or planning. T. Boone Pickens, the Texas billionaire, in an address to business school students at George Washington University, said, "Don't fall victim to what I call the 'ready — aim — aim — aim — aim syndrome.' You must be willing to fire."

North Carolina's late senator, Sam Ervin, was a delightful wit. He once told the story of John and Mary sitting on a bench in the moonlight. The fragrance of the flowers filled the air, and everything was conducive to romance. John asked Mary, "If you wasn't what you is, what would you like to be?"

Mary replied, "An American Beauty Rose." She turned the question on him: "John, if you wasn't what you is, what would you like to be?"

John responded, "An octopus."

"Why?" asked Mary.

"Because an octopus has eight arms, and I would put every one of them around you," answered John.

Mary said, "Stop your foolish talk. You ain't usin' the two arms you got."

Hearing and doing. Those who have ears....

The Transfiguration Of Our Lord
(Last Sunday After Epiphany)
Matthew 17:1-9

What Boggles Your Mind?

The day had started off ordinarily enough — Jesus and his three closest friends went up on a high mountain. Nothing unusual. Jesus often went off from the crowds to pray and rest. Nothing particularly mind-boggling about that.

But from there on, the boggling began in earnest. No sooner did they arrive, than Jesus was suddenly "transfigured." He "glowed." As the text has it, "His face shone like the sun, and his clothes became as white as the light." Wow! And if that is not mind-boggling enough, two of faith's most honored dead guys suddenly appeared by Jesus' side. Moses, the great law-giver, and Elijah, the prophet par excellence — the Law and the Prophets — paying respect to Jesus, in whom both are brought together. This is both literally and figuratively a "mountaintop experience." No wonder Peter, James, and John were terrified.

Of course, a little terror never stopped Peter from speaking up; for lack of any other ideas, he suggested erecting three shelters to commemorate the event, but the scripture reads that before he could even finish speaking, God interrupted and said, "Listen." Big-time boggle! It was so extraordinary that when it was all over, and Jesus and Peter and James and John were headed back down the mountain, Jesus told them, "Don't tell anyone what you have seen." That made sense. Who would have believed it anyway? But the three of them believed it. They had been there, and those moments on that mountain would forever mark their lives and change the way they looked at everything. Certain mind-boggling moments have a way of doing that.

Sam Shoemaker, one of the great preachers in the first half of the last century, confessed that during his seminary days, as he studied and reflected on God and creation, he found it difficult to imagine how the Lord could even think about these little specks of life called human beings. How could God have time for us when there was so much more to demand the divine attention? Shoemaker explained his thoughts to one of his professors, an eminently wise man. "Mr. Shoemaker," he said, "your problem is that your God is too small. God takes care of the sun, the moon, and the stars with just a word. Now, God has all the time in the world just for you and me." Mind-boggling.

Lent

This season of Lent, which we begin today, developed gradually in the church. From what historians can tell, one of the earliest pre-Easter traditions was fasting for the forty hours between Good Friday and Easter morning. People understood that Christ was in the tomb for forty hours, so a period of fasting and remembering the sacrifice Christ made for us became part of the observance. Over time, the fasting was extended from forty hours to all of Holy Week (only one small evening meal per day would be eaten). Then, as time went farther on, the practice of observing a period well beyond Holy Week developed, and by about the year 400, the church decided on a season of Lent lasting forty days. The way of totaling the days was unusual — Sundays were not counted, since each Sunday was considered a mini-Easter celebration. Lent would begin on Ash Wednesday and end on Holy Saturday.

Why the ashes? That is an ancient custom signifying grief and mourning. In the early church, Christians who had committed grave faults were obliged to do public penance. On Ash Wednesday, the bishop blessed the uncomfortable hairshirts that they were to wear during the forty days, and sprinkled them with ashes. Then, while the faithful recited psalms, the penitents were turned out of the holy place because of their sins, just as Adam and Eve had been turned out of the Garden of Eden because of their disobedience. They did not enter the church again until Maundy Thursday after performing some act (or acts) of penance and receiving absolution. As years went on, and as the truth of the scripture sank in that says,

"All have sinned and come short of the glory of God" (Romans 3:23), all began to come to receive ashes.

To understand the season of Lent as a time of introspection and spiritual discipline, we look back to the way new converts were initiated into the early church. Lent became the special time during which new Christians prepared for baptism — instruction, sacrifice, austerity. As Easter Sunday approached, an all-night vigil would be held, and just before the sun rose on Easter morning, all those who so desired and had properly prepared were baptized in a splendid service. It did not take long for all Christians to set this time apart to recommit themselves to the faith.

We arrive at this time of recommitment once again. What will Lent mean for you this year? Consider a suggestion that may sound blasphemous in the context of Jesus' warning about public piety: "Beware of practicing your piety before others ..." This year consider being very public with your piety. Jesus wanted to guard against hypocrisy. But, the hypocrisy of our day in the mainline church is not people parading their piety to the public — it is exactly the opposite. The piety is there, but it is kept carefully private — too private. It has been noted that Christianity is always just one generation away from extinction. The faith must be shared. This Lent, take something on rather than giving something up. Be public in your piety — not for recognition, but simply to declare your faith and let the world know whose side you are on. And I can promise, God will bless you for it.

Temptation

Temptation. Every year, the gospel lesson for the first Sunday in Lent is about temptation, and the temptations of Christ in the desert in particular. What's wrong with turning stones into bread (if one can do it) to feed the hungry? Later, Jesus will turn five loaves of bread and a couple fish into a feast for 5,000. What's wrong with believing scriptures so strongly that he trusts the angels to protect him? Later, Jesus will walk on water, perhaps only slightly less difficult than floating on air. What's wrong with the King of kings and Lord of lords assuming control over the kingdoms of the world? Isn't that what we are expecting at the end of time anyway?

It is hard to imagine that so many years have gone by since Martin Scorcese's film, *The Last Temptation of Christ*, was released (the early '90s). The furor was incredible. People were horrified that the camera would suggest that Jesus had sexual thoughts or could harbor notions of abandoning his mission or have fantasies about marrying Mary Magdelene and settling down (shades of Dan Brown's *The Da Vinci Code*). There were marches and demonstrations. Remember?

One Sunday, as the congregation was filing out after the service, a well-dressed young man came to the church door, obviously looking to speak with me. In his hand he held a petition and a plan of action for me to use to help prevent the distribution or showing of *The Last Temptation of Christ*. I said, "Thanks, but no thanks." I had not seen the film and would not condemn it on the basis of hearsay evidence. I would make my *own* decision after seeing it.

He asked, "Do you want to see it?"

I said, "Of course."

I finally did see it (after it came out on video). For the most part the movie struck me as silly, but, in its own silly way, it did reaffirm the truth of scripture where we read, "He was in all points tempted like as we are, yet without sin" (Hebrews 4:15).

What tempts you? I doubt that turning stones to bread or jumping off a cliff have ever been issues. Certainly they have not been for me. Generally, I find myself tempted by good things, not evil. It is no struggle for me not to do the things that we would all agree are wrong. No, my struggle is between the good and the best. I find it so tempting to be satisfied with the status quo, which for me is pretty good. But then I am reminded of the famous line attributed to Edmund Burke two centuries ago: "The only thing necessary for the triumph of evil is for good men to do nothing."

Yes, there is evil in the world, and yes, we are always in danger of being caught in its snare, even if our only temptation is to do nothing. But we know one thing more, and this one thing is the most important of all: We are not alone in our struggle. We know beyond a shadow of a doubt that, "nothing living or dead, angelic or demonic, today or tomorrow, high or low, thinkable or unthinkable — absolutely nothing can get between us and God's love in Christ Jesus our Lord" (Romans 8:38-39 in Eugene Peterson's paraphrase, *The Message* [Colorado Springs: NavPress, 1995]). And that is good news, indeed.

The Adventure Of Faith

Life is an adventure. It starts from the very moment of birth as an infant enters a new and unfamiliar universe. The adventure continues as friends are made, schools are selected, careers are begun, and mates are chosen. Probably the greatest adventure of all comes when this life finally ends and we embark on an entirely new form of existence. Life *is* an adventure.

Life is an adventure because there is always the element of the unknown as anything new is begun. We begin new things on faith ... faith that whatever the journey happens to be, somehow it will turn out all right. For people of faith there is a certain comfort in taking adventurous steps because we believe we don't take those steps alone. As the psalmist has said, "My times are in your hands" (31:15), and we believe with all the faith we can muster that "in all things God works for the good of those who love him, who have been called according to his purpose" (Romans 8:28). For the Christian, life is no less an adventure than it is for anyone else, but there is that calm assurance that the loving God who came to us in Jesus Christ is with us on the journey ... both now and through all eternity.

Abraham believed that. God came to him and said, "I want you to pull up stakes and head out into open country. Don't worry about your destination. I will fill you in on the details as you go along." Abraham would have had every reason to say, "Wait a minute, Lord. You don't know what you're asking. I have a good life here in Haran. I am respected in my community, have a good income, and many fine friends. My wife is happy here. My father is buried here. And on top of that, I'm 75 years old. You don't know what you're asking."

But God had a plan for Abraham. The Lord told him, "I will make you into a great nation."

Of course, Abraham could have objected further. "What do you mean 'a great nation'? Up until now, you haven't even made me a great family. Here I am 75 years old and my wife is 65. We don't have any children at all, much less enough to populate a nation. Gee, Lord, maybe you're thinking of somebody else of the same name. You can't mean me! No, I don't want to move. I'll just stay right here in Haran."

Of course, to his eternal credit, Abraham did *not* say that. He did as God instructed, pulled up stakes, and began that adventure of faith that eventually did result in the founding of the people God chose to be God's own. Abraham became the paradigm of the adventurous, faithful spirit.

Years ago, Peter Marshall was reflecting on his boyhood and recalled very vividly a scene from World War I. It was during a summer vacation at a Scottish seaport. He said he saw a grey destroyer slipping hurriedly from port in response to some urgent command. He watched the crew hurry their preparations for sailing, watched them cast off the mooring hawsers, watched as the ship rose to meet the lazy ground swell of a summer evening. He watched her lamp winking on the bridge and continued to watch as she disappeared into the mists of the North Sea. She was a mystery ship. Not even her captain and crew knew her destination. She was sailing under sealed orders. What an excellent way to understand the adventure of faith.

Old Abraham lived like that. He was given, for all practical purposes, "sealed orders" to begin a journey he knew not where. So he set off, content to trust the pilot on board who knew the nature of the orders from the outset as well as the shoals and sandbars, the rocks and reefs, and finally the course to steer to find safe harbor. Do I have that kind of faith?

Jesus, Savior, pilot me
Over life's tempestuous sea;
Unknown waves before me roll,
Hiding rocks and treacherous shoal;
Chart and compass come from Thee;
Jesus, Savior, pilot me.

— Edward Hopper, 1871

Who Woulda Thunk It?

Who woulda thunk it? A Samaritan woman, having come to the village well to draw her water in the heat of the day — not early morning when the other women would come, meets a Jewish rabbi. He talks to her ... in public, even. He actually talks to her. Right out there in front of God and anybody (even though no one else is around, not in the noonday sun). This is not done. Jewish men do not talk to women in public, even their own wives. In fact, for a Jewish wife to address her husband in public without permission was grounds for divorce! But a Jewish man speaking to a mixed-breed, "racially inferior" female?

What was he doing there, anyway? The animosity between Jews and Samaritans was such that most travelers would have taken the extra nine hours to go around Samaria on a journey from Judea up to Galilee. After all, Samaritans frequently ganged up and robbed Jewish pilgrims passing through their territory, which is why Jesus' later story of the exceptional Good Samaritan would be so striking.

He asks her if she would draw him a drink of water while she is filling her pot. She is surprised and a little irritated. "How is it that you, a man, and with your Jewish accent, ask a drink from me, a woman and a Samaritan?" Fiesty. Perhaps that is why she went through so many husbands. Or perhaps that is how she survived so many husbands and the ensuing isolation coming from the ostracism of a cold-hearted village.

Then Jesus said to her, "If you knew the gift of God, and who it is that asks you for a drink, you would have asked him and he would have given you living water." What? Living water? Who is this man? He has nothing with which to draw. Is he making fun? Is he suggesting that "Samaritan water" is not good enough? So she questions, and he confuses her even more — he begins talking about eternal life. She was not sure what was happening, but she was finding herself more and more fascinated. "Sir, give me this water so that I won't get thirsty and have to keep coming here to draw water."

The conversation continues with reference to her love life and current living arrangements. This spunky lady does what we all do when Jesus wants to talk with us about our personal affairs — she changes the subject. Religion — there's a good one. She says, "I can see that you are a prophet ... clergy. Our church says worship God in this place, but your church says Jerusalem. Let's argue about that instead of talking about me." Jesus answers with the gospel for her that day and for everyone everywhere always: "A time is coming when you will worship the Father neither on this mountain nor in Jerusalem ... God is spirit, and his worshipers must worship in spirit and in truth." Cities, states, nations, and denominations are not holy. God is holy. God's people are holy. No more artificial divisions — Jews/Samaritans, Protestant/Catholic, Presbyterian/Lutheran/Methodist/Baptist — no more divisions to separate human beings one from another — good news — gospel.

The story continues as the disciples return. The woman departs, goes into the village and tells of her encounter. The people are intrigued, come out to the well and, in their words to her, "We no longer believe just because of what you said; now we have heard for ourselves, and we know that this man really is the Savior of the world." Who woulda thunk it?

To this day, that nameless Samaritan woman, the first unexpected evangelist, is revered in many cultures. In southern Mexico, *La Samaritana* is remembered on the fourth Friday in Lent, when specially flavored water is given to commemorate her gift of water to Jesus. The Orthodox know her as *Saint Photini*, or *Svetlana* in Russian. Her name means "equal to the apostles," and she is honored as apostle and martyr on the Feast of the Samaritan Woman.

Telling The Story

The account of the healing of the blind man in our gospel lesson is wonderful. He meets Jesus. His life is changed. His friends see the difference. Finally, he is asked to give a theological perspective to the incredible event, but he refuses. All he finds necessary to say is "One thing I do know. I was blind but now I see!" The story is sufficient.

This is marvelous instruction about evangelism. Tell your own story. Will people be interested? Yes, indeed. As they confront realities like earthquakes and hurricanes, fires and floods, plus the myriad of other personal disasters that occur, they wonder, "Where is God in all this?" As has been said, there are no atheists in foxholes. People are interested in talk about God.

For those worried about doing it correctly, the word is *don't*! God uses the most imperfect storytellers to get the message across. The Lord works in mysterious (and sometimes mischievous) ways.

The task of evangelism is a daunting one in the mainline church in our day. Despite the fact that Gallup polls consistently show that Americans are exceedingly religious (generally about 95% claiming a belief in God), recent statistics on the number of unchurched people in this nation make America one of the largest mission fields in the world. With Isaiah, we long for the day when everyone will stream to the Lord's house to learn God's ways, to walk in God's path, beating swords in plowshares and spears into pruning hooks (Isaiah 2:2-4). We long for a day when oppression and injustice will be no more. Combine that with the decline in ethical and moral standards among our young and we begin to understand the urgency of the mission.

The enormity of the undertaking might be daunting, but I find help in something I read once from former Oregon Senator Mark Hatfield who reported on a conversation he had with Mother Teresa at her hospital in Calcutta. After having seen the incredible task she faced among those poorest of the poor, he asked how she was able to bear up under the load with so much to be done. She replied, "My Dear Senator, I am not called to be successful, I am only called to be faithful." It is no different with our challenge to share the gospel.

Perhaps you are familiar with the name Angelo Roncalli. You may know him better by the name he took late in life, Pope John XXIII. It is safe to say that John XXIII made more of an impact on the life of the Christian church than anyone since Martin Luther. It was John XXIII who was responsible for the sweeping changes brought about by Vatican II — a less legalistic approach to faith, worship in the language of the people, an openness to non-Catholic Christians — to name just a few. It is said that Pope John's bedtime prayer was routinely the kind of conversation between himself and the Lord that prayer ought to be. As he reflected on the events of the day, the trials and tribulations of leadership, he heard "Who governs the church? You or the Holy Spirit?" Then he would hear, "Very well then. Go to sleep, Angelo. Go to sleep."

The Ideal Pastor

"If I wanted to drive a manager up the wall, I would make him responsible for the success of an organization and give him no authority. I would provide him with unclear goals not commonly agreed on within the organization. I would ask him to provide a service of an ill-defined nature, applying a body of knowledge having few absolutes, and give him only volunteers for assistance. I would expect him to work ten to twelve hours per day and have his work evaluated by a committee of 500 people. I would call him a minister and make him accountable to God." So said Duane Swenson of the Menninger Foundation back in the days when "him" and "his" would have been perfectly appropriate in referring to a minister.

Sound familiar? It puts one in mind of the description so often given of the perfect pastor. According to surveys, he/she is 28 years old and has been preaching for thirty years. He/she is tall and short, lean and hefty, has one brown eye and one blue; hair is parted in the middle with one side blond and straight, the other, dark and wavy.

The perfect pastor works from 8 a.m. to 10 p.m. every day in every type of job, from preaching to pruning to cleaning the privys. He/she spends all his/her time with the youth of the church and visits fifteen senior citizens every day but is never out of the office when you drop by for a chat. He/she knows how to delegate authority and does all the things other people are too busy to do.

The ideal pastor wears good clothes, drives a nice car, lives in a comfortable home in a pleasant neighborhood, where he/she regularly entertains the congregation all on a salary of $100 a week, half of which is donated back to the church. Obviously, he/she understands the ins and outs of finance and develops a healthy church budget but never mentions money. His/her preaching is powerful and challenging but never steps on anyone's toes and, of course, never goes on for more than fifteen minutes. He/she smiles all the time with a straight face because he/she has a delightful sense of humor that keeps him/her serious about the work.

He/she has a wonderful spouse and fun-loving, well-adjusted children who never seem to mind that Dad/Mom is always busy with other people's needs. He/she is a warm, compassionate, deeply caring person but whose own skin is so thick that no unkindness or insult has any negative effect.

We laugh at that sort of description but the laughter has just a bit of an edge to it because those wild expectations are not entirely far-fetched. The result has been a presumption in recent years that ministers are an unhappy lot and that significant numbers are leaving to find other employment. But according to findings in the Pulpit & Pew National Clergy Survey, seven out of ten who responded say they have never considered leaving the ministry and are happy in their vocation.

Truth be known, it is an incredible vocation if one is called to it. There are wonderful satisfactions among the challenges. We can identify with Ezekiel's imagery. The prophet stands before a vast panorama of desolation ... an ancient valley full of parched skeletons, baked in the desert sun for who knows how long. The grim reaper had had a field day.

Now a conversation. God says, "Tell me, Son, will these bones ever come back to life?" The prophet responds, "C'mon, Lord. You know the answer to that — when you're dead, you're dead." To which God answers, "Preach to them, Son. Tell them that I will bring them back!" A wonderful word of hope from Ezekiel to those exiled Israelites who were afraid their best days were behind them and they would never get back home. And a wonderful word for occasionally frustrated preachers who wonder whether their work and words ever make a difference. The text says good preaching can even raise the dead.

So I preached as I had been commanded; and as I preached, suddenly there was a noise, a rattling, and the bones came together, bone to its bone. I looked, and there were muscles on them, and flesh had come upon them, and skin had covered them; but there was no breath in them. Then God said to me, "Preach to the breath; Preach, Son, and say to the breath: 'Thus says the Lord GOD: Come from the four winds, O breath, and breathe upon these dead ones, that they may live.'" I preached as God commanded me, and the breath came into them, and they lived, and stood on their feet, a vast multitude. — Ezekiel 37:7-10

When a local preacher died, his relatives found he had neatly tied up the messages he had delivered and placed a card on top of them with this inscription: "Where has the influence gone of all these sermons I have preached?" Underneath he had scribbled in large letters, "over." On the other side this answer was found: "Where are last year's sunrays? They have gone into fruits and grain and vegetables to feed humankind. Where are last year's raindrops? Forgotten by most people, of course, but they did their refreshing work, and their influence still abides. So, too, my sermons have gone into lives and made them nobler, more Christlike, and better fitted for heaven."

"I preached as God commanded me, and the breath came into them, and they lived, and stood on their feet, a vast multitude."

A Drama In Three Acts

Philippians presents the story of Jesus as a drama in three acts. It begins before recorded time and presents him with all the attributes and powers ... the "form" ... of the mighty God. We know little about that period except for sketchy references here and there in scripture, which make plain that the Jesus we came to know on the hills of Galilee had long before been involved in the creation of those hills.

But the drama continues and in Act Two, Christ gives up ... "empties" himself ... of many of the attributes of God, and assumes human form. How are we to understand that? How could Jesus empty himself of his divine powers and still be divine? Try an analogy. Think of how fathers and sons play baseball through the years. When the boy is just a tyke, the two could play catch, Dad throwing the ball underhanded, the lad catching it ... occasionally. The youngster then whips it back to Dad (or at least in his general direction) and Dad catches it or goes after it. There is no way the two could ever enjoy playing catch together had Dad thrown the ball with all the power at an adult's command. But for the sake of the boy, Dad "empties" himself of his full power. The power is still his; he just would not use it.

"He emptied himself, taking the form of a slave, being born in human likeness." This is the part of the story with which we are most familiar even though we know little about the details of Jesus' life. Jesus left no record. He kept no diary. He wrote no book. All that we know about him is crowded in a few pages at the opening of the New Testament. It can be read through in a few hours.

70

The story opens with the birth of a baby in an out-of-the-way town called Bethlehem with his first cradle a manger for the feeding of livestock. He grew up in the unsanitary mountain village of Nazareth known only for the fact that nothing "good" had ever come from that town. He learned the trade of a carpenter, but at about thirty years of age, he laid aside the tools of his trade and began to teach and preach and heal. People responded, some positively, some not. He had hardly begun his work when he was arrested on suspicion of leading a popular revolt and was condemned to an outlaw's execution. "... obedient to the point of death — even death on a cross." The life that had begun in humble obscurity ended in public shame.

Of course, the story of Jesus did not end with his death and burial. The curtain on Act Three of the divine drama began on Easter morning ... resurrection. That Jesus did survive death seems to me convincingly proved. How else can we account for the fact that eleven men in hiding, terribly disappointed and disillusioned, frightened for their lives to the extent that they were afraid to meet without first locking doors, suddenly became fearless missionaries? Peter shouted to a crowd of thousands in Jerusalem just six or seven weeks after the crucifixion, "God raised him from the dead ... of that we are witnesses." Were it not true, someone in the crowd would have yelled back, "Don't be silly. I can take you to his body right now." Of course, no one did. But the resurrection was only the beginning of Act Three in this divine drama. God raised Christ, not only from the dead, but once more to the heights and gives him a name above every name. God gives him the name Lord!

Jesus Christ is Lord! That is where the whole faith came together for those early Christians. Through the years that followed, the church would debate how Jesus was both God and man at the same time, there would be discussions about how to understand the Trinity, and there would be arguments about methods of baptism and serving the Lord's Supper. To this day, the church finds things to fight about. But the one thing the church said at the beginning is still being said today: that Jesus of Nazareth was the Son of God and now is the mighty Lord of the universe. It is the simplest creed imaginable — the creed before creeds. Jesus Christ is Lord!

Maundy Thursday
John 13:1-17, 31b-35

The Upper Room

I've been there, the upper room, where this scripture is set. Or at least I've been to the place in Jerusalem that tradition and all the tourist bureaus *say* is the upper room. As I recall, the building is in the southwest portion of the city. On the ground floor these days is a *yeshiva* ... a Jewish seminary/school. Visitors ascend an outdoor staircase then enter the room on a landing from which four or five more steps lead down to the stone floor. It is a large, light, airy room with a high, vaulted ceiling supported by several ornately decorated arched pillars strategically placed.

My one and only visit was as leader of a small group of parishioners and friends who were touring the holy land some years ago. It was a fascinating trip. So many of the decisive moments in world history have taken place on that sandy, blood-soaked soil. For people of faith, a visit helps to bring to life the stories we began learning from our youngest childhood. I read familiar passages and think, "I've been there."

We had been warned ahead of time about our visit to the upper room. You see, clever tour leader that I was, it had occurred to me how meaningful it would be for our group to celebrate the Lord's Supper in this space where Jesus and the twelve may very well have partaken on the night before the crucifixion. Of course, every other preacher-leader has the same inspiration. So, long ago, the tourist authorities in charge of the building said, "No way, never!" Too bad.

Our little band arrived in the room just as another group of Christian tourists was concluding their visit. Wait a minute. It was obvious they had just shared the bread and cup — a special moment. There was a joy on their faces that was a positive glow. But ... but, but we had been told.... As they made their way out, I asked our Israeli tour guide who had been the one who had previously informed us of the "No Communion" rule what was going on. She said the rule still stood and was vigorously enforced ... mostly. The only reason that the previous group got away with their service was that they were Pentecostals ... hands in the air, faces toward heaven, eyes closed in religious ecstacy. The Pentecostals could get away with anything they wanted because the authorities were afraid of them. They thought these folks were all crazy; who knew what mayhem might ensue if anyone got them upset? Well, okay. I've been there, too ... not with my Pentecostal friends, but there have been people I would avoid if at all possible, not wanting to say or do anything that would make them crazier than they already were.

I wonder if Jesus ever felt that way. I doubt it, otherwise he would have been more selective in his choice of friends. After all, the twelve were *not* your normal dozen or so who would have gravitated together under any other circumstance. Some, perhaps: Peter, Andrew, James, John — fishermen ... that would be a common bond. But even among them, there had been an argument about who would hold the most favored positions in the coming kingdom. Add someone like Matthew — a tax collector — someone who was thought of as a traitor to his own people, willing to sell himself in the service of Rome. Then, put Matthew in the same room as the other Simon, the Simon who is identified in scripture as the Zealot, a man whose politics hated anything Roman and advocated the violent overthrow of the government, and we have a war waiting to break out right there under those arches. The story of Jesus washing everyone's feet at the beginning of the meal is just one more clue to this group. Foot washing was the task of the lowliest house servant, and since none of the twelve would be bothered to stoop to such a level, Jesus took on the duty himself. What a group!

We should not be surprised, though. This does sound like a crowd that Jesus would bring together. You remember the complaints the religious folk had about him — he ate with the wrong people ... "tax collectors and sinners" was the phrase! They knew back then, just as middle schoolers in the cafeteria know today, that we are known by those with whom we share a table. But, share a table he did, and ever after, we have all been welcome to join the feast: rich and poor, sick and healthy, sinners and saints. No limits. Anyone who is willing to be a friend. Wonderful. Thank God, I've been there, too!

The story does not end with that, though. If it did, we might remember this as Communion Thursday or even Foot-Washing Thursday. But we call it Maundy Thursday, the *maundy* coming from a Latin word meaning commandment. This, first and foremost, is *Commandment* Thursday: Jesus says to his friends, "I give you a new commandment, that you love one another." When you consider that bunch who first heard this instruction, you realize that these are not just warm-fuzzy words. Jesus' demand is that the differences be put aside, natural alliances be discarded, pet peeves be shelved, and politics be left at the door. This is not easy. But what should we think? Should the Lord expect less of his friends? Of course not. He expects the *best* from us.

That group of twelve managed ... amazingly. They did put aside their differences. They gathered around Jesus. They were energized. And despite all they would go through in coming days, the bond of fellowship that was cemented at the table held tight. They went out from that upper room and changed the whole world.

The Blame Game

There is something in us that likes to assess blame. We like answers. We want conclusion. Mel Gibson's movie, *The Passion of the Christ*, raised the issue concerning the crucifixion of Jesus. Some who saw the film thought Mel's answer was that the Jews killed Jesus. Thus, the complaint began that the film was anti-semitic. In a sense, the charge is legitimate — after all, Gibson says that the major source for the script is the gospel accounts themselves, and the truth is that the gospels can also legitimately be charged with being anti-Jewish.

The truth is that most Jews of Jesus' day had never heard of him and could have cared less whether he lived or died. Some knew of him and became followers. Some knew of him and became concerned, the most notable being the leaders of the temple. They were afraid this rabble-rousing rabbi who went around talking about the "kingdom of God" was going to rouse the wrath of the empire of Caesar, or at least Caesar's hand-picked governor, Pontius Pilate. After all, Pilate was immensely powerful, with even the high priest only serving at the governor's pleasure. To get on his bad side would have been most hazardous, not only to career, but probably to health as well.

It was Passover time in Judea, and a mob from all over the known world would be assembling in Jerusalem. It has been described as Times Square on New Year's Eve, but for two-and-a-half straight weeks and without sanitation. Pilate had come to Jerusalem from his normal residence in a palace by the sea. He only came up at Passover time because there was such an opportunity for civil unrest and he needed to be ready. There had previously been a Passover riot that he had had to put down with a massacre (Luke 13:1). Pilate would not have been a happy camper.

The Jewish leaders had come to Pilate with this one they said was a danger. And to their credit, they genuinely believed it. Here was a man who attracted large crowds; he had made a wreck of the temple courtyards, turning over the tables of the moneychangers and sellers of sacrificial animals, all of whom had their jobs by being related to these same leaders. This "kingdom of God" talk was politically dangerous. The high priest was the one whom Pilate would hold responsible for any civil disorder, especially at Passover. This was enlightened self-interest; that is why Caiaphas would say privately, "it is better ... that one man die for the people than that the whole nation perish" (John 11:50).

Ultimately, the decision was Pilate's. Mel Gibson's film presented the governor as something of a philosophical humanitarian, which is based on only the tiniest passing references in scripture. The Apostles' Creed gets it right when it states that Jesus "suffered under Pontius Pilate." Pilate was boss; he wielded absolute authority in Judea. The Roman legion, the army of occupation, answered directly to him; and that meant so did everyone else. Crucify Jesus? No big deal. That was a punishment routinely handed out to troublemakers. Who knows how many others suffered that fate under Pilate? He was a brutal tyrant who had no moral qualms about executing anyone he perceived to be a threat.

So why do the gospels treat the man relatively gently? It has to do with something that occurred, not at the time of Jesus' death, but rather something almost forty years later. In the year 70 AD — just before the three gospels of Matthew, Mark, and Luke were written, and a decade or two before John — the Roman general, Titus, marched his legions through Jerusalem, massacred tens of thousands of Jews, burned most of the city, and pulled down the temple, stone by stone. It was Jerusalem's 9/11, a first-century holocaust. No wonder the gospel writers were not anxious to assess blame on Rome; that might have been the end of them.

So how do we choose the winner of this "blame game"? First, we can say that the Jews as a people did not do it, despite what certain passages in the gospels, taken out of context, could lead us to believe. Was it the high priests? Not really. They lacked the authority. Pilate? He would appear most culpable.

But for us, on this holy day, as we recall the horrific events of Calvary, we look at the total witness of scripture and are forced to say, "I did — I killed Jesus!" We hear again the witness of the prophet Isaiah thundering over the centuries before, "he was pierced for our transgressions, he was crushed for our iniquities; the punishment that brought us peace was upon him, and by his wounds we are healed. We all, like sheep, have gone astray, each of us has turned to his own way; and the Lord has laid on him the iniquity of us all."

We can debate Mel Gibson over the way he made *The Passion of the Christ*, but in one respect he had the right idea. Do you know whose hand portrays the Roman soldier pounding the nails into Jesus' flesh? Mel Gibson's. Any extra could have played that role, but Gibson chose to do it himself. Ask him the question then, who killed Jesus? Ask me. Ask yourself.

"I did. I killed Jesus."

Rolling Stones

The story is certainly familiar. It should be — fully one-quarter of the material we have in the gospels is dedicated to it. In the pre-dawn darkness of the first day of the week, some of Jesus' most devoted friends — women — made their way to the garden of Joseph of Arimathea, to the tomb where their Lord had been laid after being taken down from the cross. The embalming process had begun on Friday afternoon, but, because of sabbath restrictions against work, it could not be finished until now. So here are the women, ready to complete their somber task.

Foolish women. What about the stone? In front of the opening to the tomb was a groove in the ground; and in the groove ran a huge stone, circular like a cartwheel; and the stone had been wheeled into position to close the opening. In fact, the authorities had actually sealed that stone to make sure that no one would move it. What's that you say? The stone was rolled away? Yes. As we say, the story is familiar.

A church school teacher has told of an Easter pageant she staged with her class. When it came time to assign parts, some children wanted to be soldiers, others the women at the tomb, still others the apostles. One little boy, however, insisted on playing the stone that was used to block the door of the tomb. No speaking part? "No," said the little boy, "I want to be the stone." The teacher asked why. "Because it will feel so good to let Jesus out of the tomb." Smart kid.

Have you ever wondered about that stone? A stone is a stone is a stone. Big deal. Yes, this one *was* a big deal — probably a couple hundred pounds ... more than the average woman (or even two or three) could move. The Easter story says many things, and one of them is that our God, in addition to everything else, is in the business of "rolling stones."

Newsweek magazine (3/2/99) reported in a cover story concerning the continuing influence of Jesus, the response to a question posed by a survey: "Do you believe that Jesus Christ rose from the dead after dying on the cross?" 88% of Christians said, "Yes"; 32% of *non*-Christians also said, "Yes"! Almost one-third! What should we make of that? Perhaps that folks who have seen one miracle after another in the world of quantum physics and microprocessors are less astounded at the fact of physical resurrection than we might suppose. The new question then becomes, "So what?" Does Jesus' resurrection have anything to do with me? Can it fill my emptiness and dry my tears? Can it change my life?

The answer may be as near as that stone, the one that is stopping you from really living. That *big* stone.

Does your stone have a name? Perhaps it is guilt. Something you have done or failed to do is haunting you. The first disciples must have felt it ... they had let Jesus down horribly. But Easter came and the stone was rolled away. Is your stone named guilt? Lord, come again, and roll away the stone.

Perhaps your stone is fear. The first disciples felt it ... cowering behind closed doors. But Easter came and rolled that stone away, too ... opening the path to a fearless faith. Is your stone named "fear"? Lord, come again, and roll away the stone.

Perhaps your stone is weakness, something that has taken control of you that will not let loose. Yes, the disciples felt helpless and hopeless, too. But Easter came and rolled it away and they were remarkably changed. Is your stone named "weakness"? Lord, come again, and roll away the stone.

Your stone may have many names. The good news of this resurrection morning is that our God is a God of rolling stones. Lord, come again, and roll away the stone.

God's Ultimate Cosmic Joke

Many congregations have begun celebrating this second Sunday of Easter as Holy Humor Sunday. It is based on the understanding that the resurrection of Jesus is God's ultimate cosmic joke on all the forces of evil and death. We bring bells and noisemakers to worship and use them heartily at any points in the service that reflect celebration: "alleluia," "praise," "rejoice." The resurrection is comedy of the best sort, the unexpected reversal of expectations. Mary comes to the tomb on Easter morning expecting to find a dead body. Her train of thought keeps barreling along one track, and she almost literally stumbles over the risen Lord. Humor of the highest order. Resurrection reverses the expectation of gloom and doom in the face of death and instead brings celebration. Party time! Blow the horns! Ring those bells!

Doesn't sound much like church, does it? Oliver Wendell Holmes once said, "I might have entered the ministry if certain clergymen I knew had not looked and acted so much like undertakers." Robert Louis Stevenson once entered in his diary, as if he was recording an extraordinary phenomenon, "I have been to church today, and am not depressed." Amazing!

Tom Mullen, a modern theologian of laughter, wrote a book with the intriguing title, *Seriously, Life is a Laughing Matter* (Waco, Texas: Word Books, 1978). Tom takes on that common vision of religion as restrictive, punitive, and dour that implies that Christian faith is like going to the dentist — if it is good for us, it is supposed to hurt. Tom disagrees. So do I.

First Peter disagrees, too. "Praise be to the God and Father of our Lord Jesus Christ! In his great mercy he has given us new birth into a living hope through the resurrection of Jesus Christ from the dead, and into an inheritance that can never perish, spoil, or fade — kept in heaven for you, who through faith are shielded by God's power until the coming of the salvation that is ready to be revealed in the last time. In this you *greatly* rejoice, though now for a little while you may have had to suffer grief in all kinds of trials."

Yes, there are trials. We know that. The news is full of them. The trials might be personal and private as jobs disappear, children disappoint, or families fail. But the word of God says those trials are not the last word. Salvation is.

Salvation is a "churchy" word that is often misunderstood as pie-in-the-sky, by-and-by— salvation equals fire insurance. The word comes from a Latin root, *salus*, which has nothing to do with life after death; it means "health" or "wholeness." It is very similar in meaning to the Hebrew word *shalom* that folks over-simplify in translation as "peace" because it, too, carries the idea of wholeness. And it begins here and now. Study after study insists that a positive mental outlook, an optimistic view of the future is crucial to health and wholeness — salvation. That means salvation has already begun. We can have all the confidence, all the optimism anyone would ever need because we know how the story finally ends — not with the whine of missiles or the whimper of war-ravaged children, but with the "tidings of great joy," first heard over Bethlehem and the Hallelujah chorus sung by the hosts of heaven. Rejoice! We have all the reason in this world ... and the next one, too!

I like the way the lesson closes: "Though you have not seen him, you love him; and even though you do not see him now, you believe in him and are filled with an inexpressible and glorious joy, for you are receiving (*present tense*) the goal of your faith (*and what is that?*) the salvation of your souls."

A. W. Tozer, that great preacher of a previous generation, was right. Perhaps we Christians *can* be seen as a bit odd: We love someone we have never seen; we daily speak aloud to someone we

81

do not hear. We are strongest when we are weakest and richest when we are poorest. We die so that we might live and give away so we can keep. We see the invisible, hear the inaudible, and know that which is beyond knowledge. Christian. Strange? No. We just know the end of the story, and that makes all the difference.

East Of Easter

Easter is past, and if you can think of that momentous event as midnight on a clock, the beginning of a new day in human history, then superimpose a compass over that clock, we are *east* of Easter. That should mean something. Think about it as we reflect on those two friends we meet in the gospel lesson.

They were just like us. They had the same concerns that have been common in every age — keeping body and soul together, keeping out of trouble, keeping up with the Joneses, keeping in tune with the times, and now keeping a stiff upper lip in the face of dashed hopes and shattered dreams. Just like us.

They were religious folk, having walked the several hours to Jerusalem a few days before from their home in Emmaus. With a real sense of excitement, they had gone to the holy city — obviously for the Passover, an event no good Jew could miss; but also to be near Jesus, one whom they had come to look on as Israel's deliverer, the Messiah. But now they were going home ... dejected, depressed, and defeated.

As they walked, they talked. Probably about mundane things: taxes too high, wages too low, children too wild, probably a little about the trial and crucifixion, but nothing too much — too hurtful. Small talk to survive large pain. We all do it, until forced to do otherwise.

Perhaps that is why Jesus engaged them in conversation. The Great Physician was also a Great Therapist. These two *needed* to verbalize what was inside, to get things out, to let some air get to the psychic wound. They were still living *west* of Easter, where "the world, the flesh, and the devil" come out on top. They needed to see for themselves that the new day had dawned.

With a sadness tinged by anger, they described the events that had made them so heavy of heart — their disappointment with respected religious leaders, their distress at the political system that could be so easily manipulated by evil men, and their despair at the loss of someone who had personified their hope for the future. Sounds very much like something in tomorrow's newspaper. Those things happen in any age. But there was something different here. Along with all the rage they were venting, they had that strange story they had heard from some women friends about an empty tomb, a vision of angels, and a risen Lord.

Fortunately, their companion had the answers. Did the travelers understand? Not quite. But now they had arrived in Emmaus. The afternoon had gone too quickly; they did not want their conversation to end. "Friend, can you stay for a bite of dinner? We don't have much — just some bread and wine — but we would love to have you. Won't you stay, please?"

In the King James Version of scripture, which nurtured many of us, the invitation of the two travelers reads, "Abide with us; for it is toward evening and the day is far spent," words that were the inspiration for that beloved hymn, "Abide with me / Fast falls the eventide." The hymn was written by Henry Francis Lyte, for 25 years the vicar of the parish at Devonshire, England. He was 54 years old, broken in health, and saddened by dissensions in his congregation. On Sunday, September 4, 1847, he preached his farewell sermon and went home to rest. After tea in the afternoon, he retired to his study. In an hour or two, he rejoined his family, holding in his hand the manuscript of his immortal hymn.

Lyte's "eventide" has nothing to do with the end of the natural day but rather the end of life. "Swift to its close ebbs out life's little day / Earth's joys grow dim, its glories pass away." The words are about the faith that faces life and death fearlessly and triumphantly in the light of the cross and the empty tomb ... east of Easter. Thus Lyte could conclude, "Heaven's morning breaks, and earth's vain shadows flee / In life, in death, O Lord, abide with me." Vicar Lyte died three months later.

Jesus accepted the invitation of the two friends on the road, of course, just as he accepted the invitation of Henry Lyte. Jesus always accepts. And during the course of that simple Emmaus meal, as the gospel record has it, "their eyes were opened." Did they suddenly have all the answers? Of course not. But they had a glimpse now of the future ... God's future ... a future to be faced with confidence.

The Shepherd Psalm

The Shepherd Psalm appears on this Fourth Sunday of Easter every year. No doubt, it is the world's most favorite passage of scripture. It is used almost automatically at funerals: "Yea, though I walk through the valley of the shadow of death, thou art with me." That is the rendering from the King James Version that many of us memorized. More modern translations have it different (differences that have prompted some folks to ask, when it comes time for their funerals, please read the old, *familiar* words).

There are other differences too, for instance, that we do not find, "He leadeth me in paths of righteousness," but instead, "He leads me in right paths" (NIV). No "valley of the shadow of death," rather "the darkest valley" (NIV). The modern translators chose these English words because they are truer to the original Hebrew. And as we pay attention to the difference these changes make, some of this confused logic begins to straighten out, and a whole new picture of this psalm emerges.

Bernard Anderson, who taught Old Testament at Princeton Seminary for years, suggests that we imagine the narrator is not picturing himself as a sheep, but as a lost and lonely traveler. The blazing heat of the desert noonday is long gone, and the bitter cold of desert night is coming fast. The road has disappeared into the twilight. Provisions of food and water ran out hours ago, and the traveler is parched and hungry. In the distance, a jackal howls. Fears of wild animals and bands of robbers invade his mind. He regrets having begun this journey, and wonders if it will be his last.

But then the traveler sees a figure on a hillside, outlined against the darkening sky: a shepherd — a common, ordinary man, but one who knows these hillsides and ravines. He goes down to the weary traveler, and leads him up out of the shadowy valley to a place where the last beams of sun still light the way ahead. He leads the wayfarer to a grassy meadow, and invites him to lie down and rest a while. The shepherd cups water from the oasis spring in his hands, and offers it. The traveler drinks and drinks and drinks.

He glances up to see the shepherd's rod, the dangerous-looking club with which he protects the sheep, and his staff, or walking stick. It is comforting to see these symbols of a man who knows his way through the desert.

When the traveler has rested a bit, the two walk on, following "the right paths" this time, to a black goatskin tent set amidst an encampment of other tents. These are bedouins, dwellers in the dry and desolate places, determined people who know how to scratch a living from the desert. They are also outsiders to the rest of society, even outcasts. The bedouins have their own mysterious ways, unknown to our lost traveler, who would hardly have given them a thought if he passed them in the town. It occurs to him that they may even be enemies, who wish to rob or kill him.

The shepherd brings the man into his own tent. It is lit inside with oil lamps, and decorated with carpets that are as intricate and beautiful as the goatskin tent is plain. There is no fear now; the laws of Middle-Eastern hospitality are in effect. As long as the traveler is in the shepherd's tent, the shepherd is absolutely pledged to protect him from all enemies.

The two sit cross-legged at a low table, and the shepherd spreads out a meal. In a timeless gesture of honor, the host pours a flask of fragrant oil over the guest's head, and pours wine into his cup until it overflows.

The fears of night have been transformed; where there might have been aching terror, there is now serenity and trust. Such is the power of desert hospitality. Perhaps it was this hospitality that the psalmist once felt. And so moving was this experience, so unforgettable this rescue from the very jaws of death, that the writer comes to see it as symbolic of God's love. You see, in this vision, the bedouin shepherd becomes not himself as he is, but an angel of the Lord. It is somehow not he who rescues the traveler, but God. "The Lord is my shepherd ..."

Christit Our Cornerstone

"Christ is our cornerstone!" That motto was chosen over a century ago for the congregation I now serve. It was October 29, 1895, at 2:30 in the afternoon, that the grandparents and great-grandparents, aunts, uncles, cousins, the forebears of today's congregation, gathered outside in Pennsylvania's autumn chill to see the laying of the cornerstone of the church building that has been in use ever since.

For what it is worth, the natural law that insists that anything that can go wrong *will* go wrong, and at the worst possible moment, Murphy's Law, was operative even back then. According to the account reported in the *Warren Evening News* that day, the celebration originally had been scheduled for late August, but as Pastor J. W. Smith (who was serving the congregation at the time) noted in his address that day, "Things have conspired to delay us until it is now nearly the first of November." He continued, "Owing to the lateness of the season our services will be less elaborate and prolonged than they would otherwise have been." The newspaper account did not report, but we can comfortably presume, that a sigh of relief swept through the crowd.

As preachers tend to do when a congregation is gathered before them, Pastor Smith preached, and according to the newspaper, "His splendid address was delivered in his usual eloquent manner." He said,

> *An occasion of this kind suggests Christ, the chief cornerstone. This is a Christian church. It is a temple of*

Christ. May he be and ever remain its cornerstone.
There are carpets woven so that the figure permeates
the entire texture. To remove the image is to ruin the
fabric. May Christ be so interwoven with the teaching,
worship, and work of this church as to be forever in-
separable. Palsied be the hand that shall ever lift itself
in this structure to pluck a star from the crown of Jesus.
Loyalty to him is the foundation on which we build.

Eloquent, indeed.

Christ is our cornerstone. And that is not only a clever motto — that is scripture. We read it in our text from 1 Peter. But we also read, "You also, like living stones, are being built into a spiritual house to be a holy priesthood, offering spiritual sacrifices acceptable to God through Jesus Christ." That means you and I have been offered the wonderful honor of being part of this holy structure as well. We cannot be Christians without being part of Christ's church. Those who claim otherwise are simply mistaken — they can be nice people, but they cannot be Christian!

The text goes on: "But you are a chosen people" — it is no accident that we are here; the God of all the universe has brought us together; "a royal priesthood." Priests are those who offer access to God, and we do it as we open our doors to the world; "a holy nation" not "halo-over-the-head" holy, but "set apart" holy; "a people belonging to God, that you may declare the praises of him who called you out of darkness into his wonderful light."

Christ is our cornerstone — yesterday, today, and forever.

Attack Or Attract?

It has been a few years since Dan Brown's novel, *The Da Vinci Code* (New York: Doubleday, 2003), was published. From the very beginning, it got lots of attention in Christian circles because of some of the things it said about Christ and the church. For people of faith, there were uncomfortable statements, and they generated any number of articles, books, study guides, and seminars designed to debunk da Vinci.

Early on, people began asking me what I thought about *The Da Vinci Code* and what it had to say. My response from the beginning was "Read the title page." What does it say there? It says, "*The Da Vinci Code*, a novel, Dan Brown." A *novel*. Fiction. It is a great read, a wonderful airport or beach chair page turner, but it is a *novel*. Fiction. It can say all the outrageous stuff it wants. Why should we worry about that? And so I never bothered about it from the pulpit.

Then the movie came out, one that had "Blockbuster" written all over it, so some devout Christians screamed bloody murder and called for boycotts and demonstrations. Around the world, governments were asked to prohibit the showing of the film. In India, the government delayed the opening of the movie for two days until Catholic groups could be allowed a preview screening. In the Philippines, the powers-that-be slapped a "No One Under 18" designation on it, which effectively prohibited showing it in most theaters. Our local theater at the mall was picketed by folks holding signs saying that the movie blasphemed Jesus Christ. Truth is, I wonder how upset they were because they made their protest in the parking

91

lot outside the entrance while sitting in beach chairs with placards, not held high, but rather sitting on the ground and propped against their knees. Not exactly the stuff of outrage.

The story is a mystery, based on a conspiracy. There is a Harvard professor of religious symbology, an energetic French policeman, the Royal British Knight, an albino Monk-turned-assassin, and, of course, a beautiful heroine, "Sophie" whose name means "wisdom," in Greek. It is one more plot among many through the years that involve a quest for the Holy Grail, but if you have seen *Indiana Jones And The Last Crusade*, you learn here that Harrison Ford and Sean Connery had it wrong — the Holy Grail is not a cup. It is a woman, one with a huge secret that has been covered up for the last 1,700 years. The Holy Grail is Mary Magdalene, the wife of Jesus and the mother of his child.

Of course, that is not biblical. Remember, it is a novel. I, for one, am glad for anything that gets people talking about Jesus. Tom Hanks, who starred in the movie, got it right when he said, "I think the movie may end up helping churches do their job. If they put up a sign saying, 'This Wednesday we're discussing the gospel,' twelve people show up. But if the sign says, 'This Wednesday we're discussing *The Da Vinci Code*, 800 people show up.' " He is about right.

So saying, I am sorry that some well-meaning Christians have raised such a fuss. As a church, we look like petulant, selfish, angry children who throw hissy-fits anytime we don't get our own way. It smacks of the reaction that Islamic extremists had to the Danish newspaper cartoons that were not entirely reverential toward the prophet Mohammed.

The lesson in Acts recounts a visit of the apostle Paul to Athens. The city was the center of classical antiquity and home to such famous philosophers as Socrates, Plato, and Aristotle. By this point, Athens was resting on its laurels a bit (the Romans were in charge, not the Greeks), but it was still an intellectual capital, like a major university town today.

It was a religious city. In fact, Athens had more statues of gods and goddesses than all the other cities of the day combined. So here came Paul, not happy at what he saw — as the lesson has it, "he was greatly distressed to see that the city was full of idols." Perhaps he could have organized a protest in the parking lot. He had a better idea: "So he reasoned in the synagogue with the Jews and the God-fearing Greeks, as well as in the marketplace day by day with those who happened to be there." He could attack or attract ... but not both. I think he chose well.

Clouded Vision

There is an ancient apocryphal story about Jesus' arrival at the pearly gates following the ascension. The angel host was gathered to welcome God's Son and celebrate his return home after his incredible sojourn on earth. Everyone had questions and wanted to hear his story — born of a virgin, raised in humble circumstances, years teaching, preaching, healing. Eventually, there was that gruesome torture and murder, but finally the conquest of humanity's most feared enemy — death. All to share the good news of a loving God who wants nothing but the best for creation. Now the Christ is home, and everyone is exultant.

Someone asks, "Lord, now that you are no longer physically on earth, who will continue to share the good news?"

Christ responds, "There are eleven who were especially close to me, and I have given them the responsibility of getting the word out."

"O Lord, these eleven must be incredible people — the best and the brightest that creation has to offer!"

"Well, actually no," the Lord responds. "These are average folks with ordinary abilities. Not the 'best and the brightest' by any means."

"But Lord, if these are only average people with ordinary ability, how can you be sure that they will get the job done?"

"Well, to be honest," the Lord answers, "I can't be sure."

"You cannot be sure, Lord? Well, what if they fail to do the job? What is your backup plan?"

Quietly, Christ answers, "I have no backup plan."

I wonder if those standing there on the Mount of Olives over-looking the holy city had any idea that there was no "backup plan." I suspect that they were not thinking much, period. After all, these past three years had been quite a ride. They had seen the teaching, preaching, and healing. They themselves had been in danger of the torture and murder. They had been witnesses of their Lord's conquest of death. These past days of close communion may well have given them the idea that things would resume where they had left off prior to the crucifixion. But such was not to be.

During the Passover Seder, prior to the Lord's arrest and trial, Jesus had said he would be moving on, but in that new scheme of things, they would be sustained by God's Holy Spirit. Now they have heard the same thing again — instructions to wait in Jerusalem and, "In a few days you will be baptized with the Holy Spirit."

Did they understand? As usual, not really. Thus the question, "Lord, are you at this time going to restore the kingdom to Israel?" In other words, "Lord, what now?"

All right, Jesus. Tell us just a bit more. We have some questions. Jesus? Jesus? As the text says, "He was taken up before their very eyes, and a cloud hid him from their sight." Hmm. It always seems to work that way, doesn't it? At the very moment we want Jesus to be most vivid, something obscures him. That is why, in some traditions, the Paschal candle that was lighted on Easter is extinguished on Ascension Day reflecting the fact that things will not be so obvious now.

Strange as it may seem, I take comfort in that. The life of faith does not lend itself to easy answers, despite what some of our friends at the extremes of the religious right and left might want us to believe. We go about our work with clouded vision, with things not always as clear as we might like ... just as the disciples did after Christ's ascension.

Perhaps the "clouded vision" is the reason for the controversy following 9/11 over whether Christians and Muslims worship the same God. According to a Harris Poll, a slender majority of Americans — 53% — believe that Jews, Christians, and Muslims all worship the same God, but 32% think they worship different gods. That is based on a nationwide sample of 2,300-plus adults. Who is right? The quick and dirty answer is both. Since both Christianity and Islam are monotheistic religions, to say that we worship different (or even competing) gods is a logical impossibility — if there is only one God, there is only one God! Thus, we worship the same God.

On the other hand, to say we have the same understanding of that God is clearly not the case. The most obvious difference is that Christians believe we come to know God through Jesus Christ; Muslims disagree.

What makes the question more pressing is our understanding of how God expects us to behave. Christians cannot imagine a God who would approve of someone flying an airplane into an office building or blowing up a crowded bus or slashing an innocent human being's head off while shouting God is great! For that matter, neither can many Muslims.

Obviously, there is disagreement within Islam as to what God expects. But to be truthful, there is disagreement within Christianity as well. Thus we have continuing controversies in the church over human sexuality, abortion, capital punishment, the role of women, and so on. We continue to deal with the same "clouded vision" as those gathered there on the Mount of Olives so long ago.

What a group! Standing there, staring into space, paralyzed like deer mesmerized by oncoming headlights. These eleven were the A-team. It was to them that the Lord entrusted his mission. There was no backup plan. But, as Will Rogers once said, "Even if you're on the right track, you'll get run over if you just stand there."

Yo! "Men of Galilee. Why do you stand here looking into the sky? This same Jesus, who has been taken from you into heaven, will come back in the same way you have seen him go into heaven." He'll be back! Meanwhile, you have his work to do.

Sounds Just Like Mom

We reflected earlier on Dan Brown's *The Da Vinci Code* and its assertion that Jesus and Mary Magdalene were married and were parents of a daughter. True, there is nothing at all in scripture to back up such a claim, but can you imagine what kind of parent Jesus would have been?

The scene in the upper room sounds positively parental. Jesus had spent the night prior to his arrest encouraging the twelve. He had washed their feet giving a lesson in humility (John 13:1-17). He had shared a bit about the future: "In my Father's house are many dwelling places ... I go to prepare a place for you" (John 14:2). He talked of their connectedness — "I am the vine, you are the branches" (John 15:1-11). There was that instruction to "love one another" (John 13:34; 15:12, 17). It was going to take that mutual support to withstand the trials and tribulation to come. Needless to say, they could not envision what their master was describing, but Jesus knew. There would be tough times ahead, and he would not be there physically with them to insure their safety. They would be on their own.

Mothers and fathers know that feeling. There is the first day of kindergarten (or pre-school, these days). Again it happens when that drivers license is newly in hand. Once more, it is felt when we unload the car with all that the new college freshman needs to stock the dorm room. Then, there is that walk down the aisle as sons and daughters begin life with someone new.

97

Jesus' prayer is that of a parent letting go of a child. Listen to some of the words again, and try to hear them as if Jesus were a dad or a mom.

Jesus says, "I have revealed you to those whom you gave me out of the world." Dad says, "I have tried to teach them properly." Jesus says, "They were yours; you gave them to me...." Dad says, "Yes, I know that my children belong to God, not me, but I know that they have been entrusted to me for a proper upbringing." Jesus says, "They know that everything you have given me comes from you." Dad says, "They have learned their lessons well."

Jesus says, "I pray for them. I am not praying for the world, but for those you have given me, for they are yours." Mom says, "Yes, I could pray some general prayer, but this is very specific and it is for my children, the ones whose welfare you entrusted to me." Jesus says, "I will remain in the world no longer, but they are still in the world, and I am coming to you. Holy Father, protect them...." Mom says, "Lord, I am not going to be there to protect them, so *you* please be there to protect them." Jesus says, "So that they may be one as we are one." Mom says, "And never let them forget that they are family!"

Jesus says, "I say these things while I am still in the world, so that they may have the full measure of my joy within them." Mom says, "Let them be happy."

Jesus says, "My prayer is not that you take them out of the world..." Dad says, "I'm not asking for any special magical treatment for them." Jesus says, "... protect them from the evil one." Mom says, "the drugs, the booze, the sex, and yes, the greed, the pride, the selfishness, *all* the ways that evil can invade and ruin a life ... Oh, God, help my babies."

Jesus says, "They are not of the world, even as I am not of it. Sanctify them in the truth; your word is truth." Dad says, "I never raised them to the standards with which the world is comfortable; I raised them by your standards. Help them to stay different based on the sure and certain knowledge that what they learned long ago is true."

Jesus says, "As you sent me into the world, I have sent them into the world." Mom says, "There was a time I left the nest; now it is their turn. Take care of them."

Jesus sounds just like a parent. Farfetched? Not really. And right now, he is doing a very parental thing — Jesus is praying for you. The Bible says so in Romans 8:34 and Hebrews 7:25. Did your folks pray for you? Do you pray for your children? Your extended family, the church? I hope so. Good moms and dads are like that — they never, ever entirely let go. Just like Jesus. And that is good news, indeed.

The Force

"May the Force be with you." Everyone recognizes that as the prayer or benediction from the *Star Wars* movies that quickly became one of cinema history's most familiar quotations. It also generated theological conversation among folks who speculated on how much Christians could identify the Force with accepted understandings of God. Most agreed that the Force left something about it to be desired, but even George Lucas himself said, "I put the Force into the movie in order to try to awaken a certain kind of spirituality in young people — more a belief in God than a belief in any particular religious system. I wanted to make it so that young people would begin to ask questions about the mystery."

A commendable goal, Mr. Lucas. For our part, the Christian church on this Day of Pentecost will go a step farther: We will identify the *real* Force. "Suddenly from heaven there came a sound like the rush of a violent wind, and it filled the entire house where they were sitting. Divided tongues, as of fire, appeared among them, and a tongue rested on each of them. All of them were filled with the Holy Spirit and began to speak in other languages, as the Spirit gave them ability."

Power! And it changed everything. Suddenly, a ragtag band of depressed disciples who had hidden themselves behind locked doors in fear for their lives became powerful public proclaimers of the resurrection. The *real* Force is with us, and that can make all the difference.

Annie Dillard, one of our most eloquent writers, has asked, "Does anyone have the foggiest idea what sort of power we so blithely invoke? Or, as I suspect, does no one believe a word of it? The churches are children playing on the floor with their chemistry sets, mixing up a batch of TNT to kill a Sunday morning. It is madness for ladies to wear straw hats and velvet gloves to church; we should all be wearing crash helmets...."[1] The *real* Force be with you.

One of the things folks remember first about that Pentecost story is the speaking in other languages. Not in some celestial language, not *glossolalia* — understandable language ... the kind that people use to communicate. The message was not just heard, it was heard ... and all this despite the fact they were speaking dozens, perhaps hundreds, of dialects and tongues. That is a miracle in itself! Not the part about the languages, but the part about hearing. It does not happen often in the world.

It happened at Pentecost. Perhaps that is one more lesson we can learn: in the church, beyond all other places in the world, we are supposed to learn to listen to one another, to value one another's feelings and opinions, as a foretaste of heaven itself, where everyone will be heard perfectly. The *real* Force is with you.

The result of all that? That little band of believers grew. They had the biggest revival any church ever saw. They exploded from being a few dozen members to adding 3,000 more that day and a couple thousand more soon after. People saw this divine "Force" in action and wanted to be a part of what was happening. Their lives were changed. The genuinely good news on this Day of Pentecost: the Holy Spirit of the living God, the *real* Force, *is* with us and will be with us ... now and forever. Hallelujah!

---

1. Annie Dillard, *Teaching a Stone to Talk: Expeditions and Encounters* (New York: Harper and Row Publishers, 1982), p. 58.

The Holy Trinity
2 Corinthians 13:11-13

Speaking Of God

Some things are difficult to talk about. Love, for example. If someone asked you to define love and explain why you love someone, how would you go about it? What if I had to explain my love for my wife? *The American Heritage Dictionary* defines love as "A deep, tender, ineffable feeling of affection and solicitude toward a person, such as that arising from kinship, recognition of attractive qualities, or a sense of underlying oneness." I could not have put it better myself ... or worse, for that matter. To be honest, no matter what I might say on the subject could never be adequate.

Here is another one: kiss. The dictionary says to kiss is "To touch or caress with the lips as an expression of affection, greeting, respect, or amorousness." Yeah. But any definition is unsatisfactory. Words will never do a kiss justice.

Try one more — God. Creator, Redeemer, Sustainer, All-powerful, Ever-present, Judge, Just, Merciful, Love, and on and on and on. Nothing is enough. Anything we might say would be inadequate.

The epistle lesson from 2 Corinthians brings us the familiar words of the traditional Trinitarian benediction, a text chosen because on the liturgical calendar today is designated Trinity Sunday, the only Sunday in the long church year that is set aside to focus on a doctrine. Christmas, Easter, Pentecost, and so on all commemorate historic events, and we can understand that, but a doctrine? And a confusing doctrine at that! Plus, as you Bible scholars well know, the word Trinity never once occurs in the pages of scripture. Why the big deal?

The doctrine of the Trinity is a uniquely Christian answer to the questions: What can we say when we want to talk about our God? What do we have? Three Gods? A committee? No — the church has always insisted there is only one. How about one big God and a couple of lesser ones? No, that means more than one again. How about one God who is revealed in three different ways: first as creator and law-giver, then as redeemer, and finally as sustainer? God would assume different roles or "modes" depending on what was needed at the moment. Sounds promising, but it leaves the dangerous possibility that someone might think of the good and loving God; the Son, coming to rescue poor you and me from the mean and angry God; and the Father, who would like nothing better than to see us roast in the fires of hell for all eternity. Not a good explanation.

The church did about all that it could do — it affirmed that, in a mysterious way, all three understandings of God are God. No way to separate any one part from another. One God who has three distinct ways of being God ... in the traditional language, "Father, Son, and Holy Spirit." To be honest, we do not even know if that is all there is to God. The Trinity is what God has chosen to reveal: It is only a glimpse. To describe the tip of the iceberg above the water is not to describe the entire iceberg. So we Christians affirm the Trinity, not as a complete explanation of God, but simply as a way of describing what we know so far.

The glimpse we have does offer us a great deal. The God we worship is the all-powerful maker of the universe. This same God is concerned not just with the whirling of the planets, but also with itsy-bitsy me and you, loving us so devotedly that scripture says even the hairs on our heads are numbered. And, if we ever wondered about God's continued presence with us, think about that hair thing and realize that, for lots of us, that total keeps changing — God has to be here just to keep up.

The message on this Trinity Sunday is simple: be careful what you say about God. Saying more than you have a right to is, frankly, blasphemous — and you do not want to go there. Remember the apostle Paul's words in the lesson: "Aim for perfection, listen to my appeal, be of one mind, live in peace ... May the grace of the Lord Jesus Christ, and the love of God, and the fellowship of the Holy Spirit — God in three persons — be with you all."

Proper 4
Pentecost 2
Ordinary Time 9
Genesis 6:9-22; 7:24; 8:14-19

Under The Rainbow

Noah and the ark. One of our earliest Sunday school memories. And yes, it must have been pretty ripe in there. Some wag has even suggested that the ark is a parable for the church: if it were not for the storm without, you could never stand the smell within!

Some years ago, Public Television ran a series called *Genesis: A Living Conversation*, hosted by Bill Moyers. The conversation about the deliverance of Noah turned to the deliverance of the survivors of the Holocaust ("Apocalypse," [Newbridge Communications, 1996]). A quote from Nobel Peace Prize winner, Elie Wiesel, was read: "April 11, 1945, Buchenwald. Hungry, emaciated, sick, and weakened by fear, Jewish inmates welcomed their sudden freedom in a strange manner. They do not grab the food offered by the American liberators. Instead, they gather in circles. Their first act as free human beings is to say *Kadesh*, glorifying and sanctifying God's name." Just like Noah. It was equally intriguing to hear that the wonderful movie *Schindler's List*, the incredible story of how one man saved hundreds of Jews from the concentration camps, was originally titled *Schindler's Ark*.

I love that old classic about the country preacher who announced that his sermon the following Sunday would be about Noah and the ark and told the congregation the scripture reference ahead of time so they might read it in preparation for worship. A couple of youngsters noticed something interesting about the page layout of the story in the church's Bibles so they slipped into the sanctuary during the week and glued two pages of the pulpit copy together.

Sunday came. The preacher began to read his text. "Noah took himself a wife," he began, "and she was ...," he turned the page to continue, "... 300 cubits long, 50 cubits wide and 30 cubits high." The preacher paused for a moment with a quizzical look on his face. Slowly, he turned the page back and read it silently then turned the page again and continued reading. Then he looked up at the congregation and said, "I've been reading this old Bible for nigh on to fifty years, but there are some things that are still hard to believe."

One of the participants in that PBS conversation with Bill Moyers was a newspaper editor. Bill asked him what would be the headline for an article that would tell the Noah story, and he responded with something like "God Destroys World." Quickly, another panelist, Samuel Proctor, that wise old retired pastor of the Abyssinian Baptist Church in Harlem, jumped in with an alternative: "God Gives Humans Second Chance!"

Sam said that he learned the Noah story from his father, a Sunday school teacher. "Sometimes we laughed at the ridiculous aspects of it ... [but] we didn't try to rewrite it. We drew from it what it said right then to the people and went on. Every Wednesday, though, my daddy would press his trousers and go down to the Philharmonic Glee Club rehearsal. These sixty black guys — table waiters, coal trimmers, truck drivers — would give one big concert a year to the white population. [We] couldn't sit where we wanted to, even though our daddy was singing — we had to sit in the back. But in the midst of all that rejection, hate, and spite, they went. And do you know the song they sang at the close of the concert? They sang, 'Yesterday the skies were gray / but look this morning they are blue.' Noah! 'The smiling sun tells everyone come / Let's all sing, hallelujah / for a new day is born / The world is singing the song of the dawn.' Sixty black guys in tuxedos in the 1920s, with lynching everywhere and hatred — 'n-----' this and 'n-----' that. But they had something we need to recover right now. I can't turn loose this story of Noah and the flood because after all of the devastation ... there's a rainbow ... I'm not going to live without that kind of hope ..."

106

The *Peanuts* characters, Linus and Lucy, are standing at the window watching the rain. Lucy says, "If it doesn't stop raining everything will be washed away."

"Oh no!" says Linus. "Genesis says that never again will God wash everything away."

"Thank you," says Lucy, "that is a great comfort to me."

Linus replies, "Sound theology will do that." No doubt.

Proper 5
Pentecost 3
Ordinary Time 10
Romans 4:13-25

God's Not Done With Me Yet!

Abraham. No individual in history is more widely recognized and revered. Abraham is patriarch to history's three great mono-theistic religions: Judaism, Christianity, and Islam. In the Bible, of all the incredible people of faith we find there, the only one called the "friend of God" is Abraham.

We learned great stories about Abraham from our earliest days in Sunday school. However, there are other stories about our hero in the Bible that probably were skipped.

For example, not long into this family journey, a famine arose in Canaan. But Abram (the original name), despite all his vaunted faith, was not so sure now, and in danger of starvation, he-and-his headed for Egypt and hoped-for relief. As they came near the border, Abe said to Sarai (which was her name before it, too, was changed), "Listen, you are one good-looking lady. If these Egyptians figure we are husband and wife, after seeing you, and wanting you, they will kill me to get to you." As Genesis has it, "Say you are my sister, so that I will be treated well for your sake and my life will be spared because of you" (12:13-20). So that is what they did: word comes to pharaoh about this foxy newcomer, he buys her from her so-called brother for his harem, Abe not only is spared but makes a huge profit — as the scripture says, "sheep and cattle, male and female donkeys, menservants and maidservants, and camels." But, pharaoh and his household suddenly began to experience one disaster after another. He traced their onset back to the arrival of Sarai, investigated, found out the deception, and confronted "Brother" Abram: "What have you done to me?" he said.

108

"Why didn't you tell me she was your wife? Why did you say, 'She is my sister,' so that I took her to be my wife? Now then, here is your wife. Take her and go!"

So Abram and Sarai and company made their exit, not only with their lives, but with all that booty as well, including one slave girl whom we hear a good deal about later. Genesis calls him "very wealthy" (13:2), but God was not done with Abram yet.

The next story you probably did *not* hear in Sunday school was of Abram, the conquering warrior (Genesis 14:1-24) — not because there is anything wrong with being a conquering warrior, but this is just not a big deal in the midst of all the other material about this famous family. It seems that some of the local kings put together a military alliance to subdue their neighbors (probably over mineral rights); in the process of the skirmish, Abe's nephew, Lot, was captured. Word came to Abram about the situation. He hastily put together a mini-army, dashed off to do battle, and quickly routed the enemy and rescued Lot and everyone else. Desert Storm #1, I guess. But God was not done with Abram, yet.

After things settled down again, our hero's heavy-duty faith began to waver a bit, and he commenced wondering about this great guarantee of beaucoups of descendants considering the fact that, at this point, he has not even *one*. God spoke to him in a vision, the promise was reaffirmed ... strangely (Genesis 15:7-21). God said, "Bring me a heifer, a goat and a ram, each three years old, along with a dove and a young pigeon." Abram did, cut them in two and arranged the halves opposite each other (but not the birds). Then buzzards tried to get at the fresh meat, but Abram shooed them off. Finally, our hero fell asleep and, as he did, God spoke to him, promising that his descendants would be given this land. As a guarantee, we have the account of an ancient ritual that would be an equivalent of "cross my heart and hope to die" — a flaming pot and a lighted torch (God is often depicted as fire) made their way between these dead animals that had been laid out and lined up. The symbolism apparently was, "May I be cut in two like all this if I fail to keep my promise!" Kind of a bloody, gory story, which may explain why Mrs. Biggerstaff did not dwell on it much when you were in Sunday school as a seven-year-old. Anyway, God is not done with Abram yet.

From here, the story may be a bit more familiar but it is still pretty sticky. As you may recall, Abram's childless wife, Sarai, in an effort to fulfill her conjugal responsibility to provide offspring, did the next best thing — she offered her husband the recreational and procreational services of her Egyptian maid, Hagar (which might make *us* blanch, but was a perfectly acceptable practice in that culture). Children were the Social Security system of the day — when you got old and were no longer able to manage for yourself, they would take care of you; it was their solemn duty. Not having any children was more than an embarrassment, it was socially and economically dangerous. So the deed was done and Hagar got pregnant.

Things got even stickier. Hagar thumbed her nose at Sarai and her barrenness, Sarai hated that. She came to Abram and complained that this was all *his* fault anyway, and insisted that Abe run Hagar off. But Abe wimped out and told Sarai to handle it herself, which she does by treating Hagar so terribly that the young maid split. As the story unfolded, the Angel of the Lord saw Hagar's predicament, came to her in her distress in the wilderness, told her to return to Abram and Sarai, have the baby, and know that God would bless him. She did, and brought forth Ishmael. But God was not done with Abram yet.

The rest is familiar. Even though Abram had a son and an heir, there was still a lot of tension in the family because the baby came from a slave girl instead of his wife. God came to our hero once again and renamed him as Abraham and his wife as Sarah and promised a son through her. Really? Abraham — Mr. Rock-solid, unwavering faith — did not simply chuckle at the thought; he fell on his face laughing at such a prospect. After all, he was 99 years old; Sarah was 89. But we know what happened. Isaac was born. Sadly, Abe allowed Ishmael and his mom to get run off by the jealous Sarah once more. As the Genesis story has it, Sarah finally died at the age of 127; Abraham married again (at around 140 years of age) and had another half-dozen children. An *active* senior citizen, to say the least. He finally died at the age of 175, "old and full of years."

A wonderful story. As the life story of Abraham attests, people of faith go through their ups and downs. Centuries later, Paul would write to the Romans concerning him, "He did not waver through unbelief regarding the promise of God, but was strengthened in his faith and gave glory to God, being fully persuaded that God had power to do what he had promised" (Romans 4:20-21). Perhaps, but Abe had his moments. How many other times do we read of someone falling on the ground and derisively laughing at what God has to say? But, of course, God was not done with him yet.

Great lesson here. No matter where Abraham was in his life, God was not done with him. God is *still* not done with him — just the fact that we are reading the story, learning from it, being inspired and guided by it proves that. Abraham and Sarah may have thought they were done ... others may have thought so too ... but not God. God is not done with me yet, either.

Proper 6
Pentecost 4
Ordinary Time 11
Matthew 9:35—10:8 (9-23)

Uncommon Laborers

Interesting collection of workers Jesus chose to accompany him — the twelve. Not a genius among 'em. Common folks: a few fishermen, farmers, even a tax collector. They were not even particularly religious. What they were was willing to be used to further the work of a man they admired, even loved, despite the fact that he was a man they misunderstood. Eventually, they came to realize (even as a few others did) that "this truly was the Son of God." And with the training they had received combined with the commitment they came to develop, those folks turned the world upside down.

Jesus said, "The harvest is plentiful but the workers are few. Ask the Lord of the harvest, therefore, to send out workers into his harvest field." Workers — not planners, not designers, not supervisors — workers. What he did not say, but what has become very obvious is that on-the-job training is available, even for the most unlikely candidates.

Flip through the pages of history and you find the picture of a man born in Italy in the twelfth century. His baptismal name was Giovanni, but the nickname Francesco — Francis — was given him and was the one by which he is remembered down to the present day, Francis of Assisi, one of the most winsome figures of Christian history.

Francis was born into the home of a well-to-do cloth merchant. He had little formal education but knew Latin and French and could read and write. His early years were spent living the life of a playboy and a reveler, destined for a career as a knight. But late in his

112

adolescence, Francis began a spiritual pilgrimage of many months, brought about by various illnesses and misfortunes. He began giving himself to the service of the poor and, despite his loathing for the disease, visited lepers and cared for them. He spent much time in solitude in the fields and hills. His fellow townspeople thought he was insane. His father became enraged at his son's behavior and locked him up in the house until his mother took pity on the young man and released him. Finally, his father took him before the local bishop to disinherit him, but Francis was undisturbed — as he stood before the bishop, he stripped off the clothes he was wearing and, now completely naked, declared that from this point onward, he desired only to serve "our Father which art in heaven."

After that, Francis left home dressed only in a ragged cloak and a belt taken from a scarecrow, feeling impelled to become a traveling preacher, proclaiming the kingdom of God and calling men and women to repentance. He was convinced that he should follow the example of Jesus and so swore himself to a life of complete poverty, subsisting on whatever food might be given him. Others were attracted by this unusual young man and began to follow him with the result that, a few years later, an order of traveling monks was established called the "Lesser Brothers" — we know that order today as the Franciscans. Francis of Assisi ... an uncommon laborer in the vineyard of the Lord.

As we flip through the pages of history, we come upon another portrait like that ... George Fox. One of the first pictures we have of him was taken in court. In 1650, a judge sentenced him to six months in jail in Derby, England, on charges of blasphemy. The youth had claimed that Christ, the Savior, had taken away his sin, and in Christ there was no sin. Before he was sentenced, George Fox told the judge to tremble in the fear of God. Professing Christ was not enough; every man must follow him. At that, the judge laughed. He knew about the meetings of Fox and his followers. People sometimes shook with emotion. So he told the young man, "You folks are the tremblers, the Quakers."

Obviously, "Quaker" was a derisive nickname, and it stuck, much the same way that the nickname "Christian" stuck some 1,600 years before at Antioch. Those people to whom the name was applied referred to themselves as "Children of the Light," or "Publishers of the Truth," or simply "Friends," following the words of Jesus, "You are my friends if you do what I command you."

George Fox was weary of formal religion. It seemed to him that the church had given up spirituality in exchange for protection from the state. Secondhand answers left the young man cold. It was not enough to read about Spirit-filled people in the book of Acts; he wanted to experience that power of God in his life. He sought advice from ministers of the day and heard things like, "Try tobacco and sing psalms." Another suggested, "Get married." Still another recommended bloodletting. Needless to say, George was a most discouraged young man. Then one day, he heard a voice. It said, "There *is* one, even Jesus Christ, who can speak to your condition." Christ was revealed to him in immediate experience. Theory became reality.

People sensed the power of God when George Fox preached. Sometimes he would speak after the minister was finished; sometimes he preached outside the church. Men argued with him. One even hit him over the head with a brass-bound Bible, upset because the brash young man knew the scriptures so well. Soon, Fox began preaching in the open air to thousands. "Christ has been too long locked up in a mass or a book," he said. "Let him be your prophet, priest, and king. Obey him." Within three years, 50,000 people had joined the Quakers and by the end of the century, there were more than twice that number.

As time went on, the Society of Friends, as they became known, challenged people to make their faith relevant to the concerns of society. The Quakers were some of the earliest and most vocal opponents of the slave trade. Since then, Quakers have been leaders in the struggle for social justice and world peace. And it all began with one young man, one uncommon laborer, one who wanted to truly follow Jesus ... George Fox.

Turn the page once more ... and find the portrait of one of the most uncommon of the Lord's laborers. Fanny Jane Crosby was born in the spring of 1820. In May of that year, just six weeks old, little Fanny caught a cold and a country doctor incorrectly prescribed a hot mustard poultice for her and it blinded her for life. At the age of five, some sympathetic friends and neighbors sent her to a noted New York surgeon to see what could be done, but his conclusion was that there was nothing. She would never regain her sight. As they prepared to leave the office, the doctor said sadly, "Poor, little blind girl!" Fanny never forgot that and determined to be thought of as more.

Fanny Crosby once told a friend that her blindness had proved to be more of a blessing than a hindrance. You see, Fanny developed a talent for writing poetry and her lack of sight enabled her to have the kind of solitude that someone needs to do that kind of work well. The result was a collection of some of the best-loved hymns in all of Christendom: "Blessed Assurance," "Jesus Is Calling," "I Am Thine, O Lord," "All The Way My Savior Leads Me," "Near The Cross," "Pass Me Not, O Gentle Savior," "Praise Him, Praise Him," and "To God Be The Glory" ... a tremendous testimony in light of her physical limitations. She even went so far to tell another friend that, if given the choice, she would still remain blind; that way, the first face she would ever see would be the face of her blessed Savior.

Fanny Crosby turned the tragedy of her infancy into the triumph of her life. She overcame terrible personal adversity to contribute a life of power and inspiration. An uncommon laborer, to say the least, but evidence that God can use us no matter what our individual handicaps might be.

"The harvest is plentiful but the workers are few. Ask the Lord of the harvest, therefore, to send out workers into his harvest field."

Proper 7
Pentecost 5
Ordinary Time 12
Genesis 21:8-21

How *Not* To Be
The Father Of The Year

It is somehow ironic that the lectionary presents this text around the time America celebrates Father's Day. It is not exactly the inspiring story of paternal love and care that we might wish for.

The story is familiar enough. Abraham and Sarah are childless, a particular disaster in the ancient world since children stabilized that society — they were a supply of labor, a promise of old-age security, and guarantors of the orderly transfer of property. Indeed, for a woman to fail to give her husband children was seen as a curse from God. But there was an alternative: surrogate motherhood. Custom of the day permitted a woman to claim as her own any children a servant girl might bear after a liaison with the master of the house. So, according to the Genesis record, with mistress Sarah's blessing (although I suspect it was given with a forced smile and through clenched teeth), Hagar became pregnant with Abraham's first child, Ishmael, a Hebrew name meaning "God hears."

It would be lovely to end it there and say they all lived happily ever after, but we know better. Sarah and Hagar hated each other. Abraham did anything he could to avoid confrontation. The boy Ishmael, even before he was born, was predicted to be all but a juvenile delinquent or a gangster (Genesis 16:12).

Between the time of Ishmael's birth and the scene in this lesson, sixteen or seventeen years had elapsed, and a major miracle had taken place. About two-and-a-half years before, at the age of ninety, Sarah had given birth to Isaac, so as far as Sarah was concerned, the faster that Hagar and Ishmael could be removed, the better.

It was at a big family party celebrating one of those rites of passage — the weaning of the child, the first step on his road to manhood, that Sarah got her chance. The Genesis account says, "Sarah saw that the son whom Hagar the Egyptian had borne to Abraham was mocking, and she said to Abraham, 'Get rid of that slave woman and her son, for that slave woman's son will never share in the inheritance with my son Isaac.' " What? For teasing the baby you get thrown out of the home? Permanent exile? Wow! Tough lady.

Father, Abraham would have shown himself worthy here of the reverence and respect shown him for centuries by three great religions. No. The story says that Abraham was displeased with the demand — after all, Ishmael *was* his son. The boy might have been a bit of a handful, but a son is a son. For whatever it is worth, Abraham was able to justify being an incredible wimp and acceding to Sarah's demand by relying on God's promise that Ishmael would also become the source of a great nation. What could the man have been thinking? "Oh, gee, Lord, that puts my mind at ease. Now, I, a wealthy man, having the wherewithal to provide handsome support, can send them out into the desert with nothing but a loaf of bread and a skin of water and not give it a second thought." Right. That *is* what he did. Bread and water and bye-bye. "See ya, Hagar. It's been fun. Bye, Ishmael. You be a good boy, now, ya hear?" Father of the year ... not.

Hagar and Ishmael wander south to the wilderness near Beersheba. The food and water are soon gone. The strength of the teenager fails first. His mother puts him under a bush, out of the blazing desert sun. As the boy sinks toward death, his mother sits down about fifty yards away and waits for the inevitable.

Ishmael starts to cry. God hears ("Ishmael," remember?) and intervenes in this story one more time. Hagar opens her eyes and sees what seems to be an oasis. A mirage? Perhaps, but waving palm trees in the desert stand out against the stark background. Hagar gathers her waning strength and goes to see. Sure enough, it is water. She fills the goatskin and takes it back to Ishmael. He drinks, his parched lips are healed. He regains his strength.

117

As the story draws to a close, we get hints of a happily-ever-after ending. They continue to live in the desert. Ishmael becomes an expert archer. His mother finds him an Egyptian wife. The only time we ever hear of Ishmael and Isaac getting together again is to bury their father (Genesis 25:9). And the bad blood between the two sides of the family continues to this day: Jews look back to father Abraham through Isaac; Arabs look back to father Abraham through Ishmael. Father Abraham ... and such a wonderful father, at that!

Of course, what we have in scripture is not to be understood as instructions on good parenting. Frankly, the models we find there, whether it be Abraham, Sarah, Isaac, Jacob, David, or whomever, are not award winners. Everyone is flawed and some of them horribly so. To be honest, these characters are just supporting cast for the real hero of the story: God. The single point of the Ishmael story is that there is no stopping God's promise. God made a promise to Abraham, and kept it. God made a promise to Hagar, and kept it. God made a promise of new life to you and me in Jesus Christ, and God will keep it. That is good news indeed.

The Second Worst Story In The Bible

What a horrible story, the second worst one in the entire Bible! True, every father at some time or other is tempted to kill his child. Like Bill Cosby's character once said, "I brought you into this world, and I can take you out." But this is not like that. What we have here is this "loving God" telling a father to stick his son like a pig, drain his blood, then set fire to the body. And Abraham goes along with it. What kind of God would ask such a thing? And what kind of parent would do it? In our own day, we know a thing or two about religious fanaticism, but this story takes it to a whole new level.

God tested Abraham ... "Take your son, your only son, Isaac, whom you love, and go to the region of Moriah. Sacrifice him there as a burnt offering on one of the mountains I will tell you about." How are we supposed to make any sense of this? Even if Abraham is not particularly heroic up to this point in the story, at least God has been. Are we supposed to believe that God someday might order one of us to kill our firstborn just to see if we are willing to do it? What kind of God would propose such a depraved test?

Then there is Abraham. No questions. No word of protest. "Sure, God. I have already lost one boy, but no matter. Whatever you say, God." Why not at least argue and bargain with God a bit like he had done in trying to preserve Sodom and Gomorrah? Needless to say, he mentions nothing of this to Sarah, because we can easily imagine what kind of a scene that would have been. He would not have had to worry about killing Isaac because Sarah would have taken her husband out first. Abraham calmly arises, saddles

119

his donkey, summons two assistants, and took his son — the only son he has left now — up on the mountaintop in search of a nice flat rock that would be suitable for human sacrifice, to satisfy what appears to be the malevolent whim of some evil deity.

This is a story that holds a most revered place in Jewish tradition. It is referred to in morning prayers and the prayers offered during the Jewish New Year, *Rosh Hashanah*. Here is the supreme example of self-sacrifice in obedience to God's will and the symbol of Jewish martyrdom throughout the ages. In Hebrew, this story is known as the *Akedah*, or the "binding" of Isaac. (Interesting that the emphasis is *not* on the testing of Abraham as we might presume.) To Jews it is a wonderful word of hope in the face of the constant threats to their collective life through the centuries. The knife is poised to strike, but then suddenly God stops it. Good news.

Early Christians also saw the *Akedah* as one of the most important of the biblical stories. It is referred to twice in the New Testament: James 2:21-24 and Hebrews 11:17-19. In both passages, what Abraham did is held up as an example of supreme faith. In the Church of the Holy Sepulcher in Jerusalem, the site where tradition says the crucifixion occurred, looking from the altar that marks the very place where the cross is thought to have stood, up at the ceiling to the right of the altar, one sees not a scene from the New Testament, but the binding of Isaac portrayed right next to the mosaic of Christ on the cross. Important story.

God tested Abraham ... "Take your son, your only son, Isaac, whom you love, and go to the region of Moriah. Sacrifice him there as a burnt offering on one of the mountains I will tell you about." Can we say Abraham passed the test? Perhaps the test was whether or not Abraham understood his God well enough to know what God really wanted. Then, yes, he passed. Go, thou, and do likewise.

By the way, if you are sitting there reading this waiting for me to wrap this all up in some neat little package, don't hold your breath. This story, as far as I am concerned, is still the second worst story in the Bible. Just remember what we have been saying from the beginning. Abraham is not the hero of this narrative, God is. And if that is the case, what are we to make of it?

Leave it at this. Move the story forward a millennium or three. The sky darkens, the wind howls, and a young man walks up another Moriah. He carries a cross on his back rather than sticks for a fire. Remember, the *Akedah* is the *second* worst story in the Bible; this one is the *worst*. And what did God do with that?

Proper 9
Pentecost 7
Ordinary Time 14
Matthew 11:16-19, 25-30

Ask The Average Person

I have some questions for the "average person." First, "Which is more important, making money or being devoted to your family?" Ask the average person that question and virtually everyone will answer, "Family," without hesitation. But watch how the average person actually lives life. See where he really invests time and energy, and he will give away the fact that he does not live by what he says he believes. He has become persuaded that if he leaves for work earlier in the morning and comes home tired at night, he is proving how devoted he is to the family by expending all that time and effort to provide them with all the things that they have seen advertised.

An ancient story is told of a king who was suffering from a certain malady and was advised by his astrologer that he would be cured if the shirt of a contented man were brought to him to wear. People went out to all parts of the kingdom after such a person, and after a long search they found a man who was really happy, but he did not possess a shirt.

Another question: "Which means more, the approval of strangers or the affection of people closest to you?" Ask the average person which means more, and she will not be able to understand why you would ask such a stupid question. Obviously, nothing means more to her than her family and her closest friends. Yet, how often have we embarrassed our children or squelched their spontaneity, for fear of what neighbors or strangers might think? How often have we poured out our anger on those closest to us because we had a hard day at work or someone else did something to upset us?

And how many of us have let ourselves become irritable with our families because we were dieting to make ourselves look more attractive to people who do not know us well enough to see beyond appearances?

One more question: "What does the average person want out of life?" The average person will probably reply, "All I want is to be happy." I believe that. I believe that most people want to be happy. I believe that they work hard at making themselves happy. They buy books, attend classes, and change their lifestyles, in an ongoing effort to find that elusive quality — happiness. In spite of all that, I suspect that most people most of the time do not feel happy. As Thoreau said, "The mass of men lead lives of quiet desperation."

Oscar Wilde once wrote, "In this world there are only two tragedies. One is not getting what one wants, and the other is getting it." He was trying to warn us no matter how hard we work at being successful, success will not satisfy us. By the time we get there, having sacrificed so much on the altar of being successful, we will realize that success was not what we wanted.

An anonymous friar in a monastery once wrote these words: "If I had my life to live over again, I'd try to make more mistakes next time. I would relax, I would limber up, I would be sillier than I have been this trip. I know of very few things I would take seriously. I would take more trips. I would be crazier. I would climb more mountains, swim more rivers, and watch more sunsets. I would do more walking and looking. I would eat more ice cream and less beans. I would have more actual troubles and fewer imaginary ones. You see, I'm one of the people who lives life prophylactically and sensibly hour after hour, day after day. Oh, I've had my moments, and if I had to do it over again, I'd have more of them. In fact, I'd try to have nothing else, just moments, one after another, instead of living so many years ahead each day. I've been one of those people who never go anywhere without a thermometer, a hot-water bottle, a gargle, a raincoat, aspirin, and a parachute. If I had it to do over again, I would go places, do things, and travel lighter than I have. If I had my life to live over again, I would start barefooted earlier in the spring and stay that way later in the fall. I would play hockey

123

more. I wouldn't make such good grades, except by accident. I would ride more merry-go-rounds. I'd pick more daisies."

There is an old *Peanuts* cartoon — Snoopy is sitting on top of his doghouse when Charlie Brown comes with a note. Charlie says, "It's a letter from your brother, Spike. 'Dear Snoopy, something wonderful happened ... a man came by here and offered to sell me a magic cape. He told me that if I wore this magic cape I would be transported to a land of paradise. He said the cape was on sale ... not wanting to miss such a bargain, I gave him my only dollar.' " The next panel shows Spike spending his time in the desert contemplating the meaning of life. Then we switch back to Charlie reading to Snoopy: "So by the time you get this letter, I'll be living in paradise." Then Spike is pictured again on the desert floor among the cactus, cape draped over his shoulders, saying, "Then again, maybe I've been had."

Too many people have been had. There are no magic capes. There is no one key that will guarantee happiness. In fact, that old aphorism about death and taxes being the only things we can count on would seem to ensure unhappiness. Ask the average person and you will hear that we live in a messed up world, a world where people fly planes into buildings, where mothers put their two-year-olds in hot ovens, a world where unspeakable horrors occur every day. There will always be low times. In fact, there will be times you get so far down that you cannot remember up. But when those times come, remember this: You are not alone. You've got a friend, one whom scripture says sticks closer than a brother — Jesus Christ — the same Jesus who issues an invitation that reaches down to us no matter how deep we are and says,

> *Come to me, all you that are weary ...*
> *all who are carrying heavy burdens ...*
> *guilt, pain, despair ...*
> *all that keeps us from being happy ...*
> *Come, and I will give you rest.*

Proper 10
Pentecost 8
Ordinary Time 15
Matthew 13:1-9, 18-23

Fertility Facts

Bible scholars tell us Matthew's gospel was compiled and distributed around 85 AD. The early church had expanded beyond Jerusalem through the missionary efforts of Paul and others but was still rather minuscule in terms of numbers and influence. There was opposition and even some persecution at the hands of political and religious establishments. It was a time when discouragement could have easily overcome that small band of believers.

These were the people for whom Matthew was writing, and this section of the gospel was organized just for them. In chapter 11, Jesus confronts political opposition as Herod arrests and murders John the Baptist. In chapter 12, he faces religious opposition as the scribes and Pharisees challenge him and even suggest he is in league with the devil himself. Now we come to chapter 13 and a series of parables. The order of arrangement is no accident — coming on the heels of these accounts of continuous opposition, the stories were meant to address that concern.

This first one, the parable of the sower, is the most familiar, (although considering the emphasis of the story, it should probably be called the parable of the soils). It uses imagery that is familiar in agricultural Palestine. It offers an automatic four-point outline. And finally, for those who fear offering an incorrect interpretation, there is (supposedly) Jesus' own explanation of the meaning of the four types of soil (but most scholars insist that the explanation is an addendum provided by a later editor).

Start with the imagery. As Jesus sat in that boat, he may well have seen a farmer off in the distance going about his work, scattering seed by hand. The field would have been one of many long narrow strips with the ground between serving as a right-of-way, a three-foot wide common path, beaten as hard as pavement by the feet of countless passers-by. If seed fell there, and some was bound to, there was no more chance of its penetrating into the earth than if it had fallen on concrete.

Then there was rocky ground, a thin skin of earth on top of an underlying shelf of limestone rock. The earth might be only a few inches deep before the rock was reached. Seed could certainly germinate, because the ground would grow warm quickly with the heat of the sun. But there was no depth of earth and when a plant sent down its roots in search of nourishment and moisture, it would meet only the rock. It would swiftly starve, shrivel, and die.

Thorny ground? Deceptive. When the sower was sowing, the ground would look clean enough. It is easy to make a garden look clean by simply turning it over, but in the ground still lay the fibrous roots of the all the perennial weedy pests, ready to spring to life again. Every gardener knows that the weeds grow with a speed and strength that few good seeds can equal. The result was that the good seed and the dormant weeds grew together, but the weeds were so strong that they throttled the life out of the seed.

Finally, the good ground, deep and clean and soft. The seed could gain an entry, find nourishment, and grow unchecked. In the good ground, the seed brought forth an abundant harvest.

Suddenly the preacher thunders, "And what type of soil are you?" (Isn't that the way it is supposed to go?) First, there are those whose minds are shut, those into whom the seed of an idea has no more chance of taking root than the seed that falls onto a path beaten hard by many feet. Is that you? Then there is the one whose mind is like the shallow ground, someone who follows the fads, responds to the emotion of the moment, who takes something up quickly and just as quickly drops it. Is that you? Or there is that busy, busy, busy individual who has so many irons in the fire, so many interests in life, that often the most important things get crowded out. Is that you? Finally, the good ground, the fertile mind

— like good soil, it is open, deep, and uncluttered. A word from the Lord will take root there and bear an abundant harvest. Is that you?

Well, to be painfully honest, I am *all* of them. There are times when someone speaks to me that they may as well be talking to a wall. For whatever reason, I do not hear what they are saying. The seed is falling on the path. There are times when an idea comes that I latch right on with enthusiasm but there is no follow-through. It dies away, as on rocky ground. My life is busy, as is yours. Everyone knows we have far less leisure time than we used to. Good ideas come, and they begin to take root, but with so many competing claims on me, they fade and eventually wither. Thorny ground. Finally, yes, there are times when something comes along that takes root — it grows and blossoms and produces abundantly. I wish that such were always the case, but....

Frankly, we could listen to 1,000 sermons on these soil types and still be the same mixtures as we are — part and parcel of being human. That is one of the things that convinces me that Jesus had something else in mind when he told this story.

Another is the placement of the parable in the gospel narrative. This is right after accounts of opposition, and the first in a series of vignettes that describe the sure and certain victory of the kingdom of God.

One more thing convinces me: Jesus was a good storyteller, and good storytellers know that you cannot make a multitude of points in a story and have any hope of your listeners remembering them. Jesus had a point to make here, not a whole list of them.

For Matthew's audience of good church people who, for various and sundry reasons, might be a bit discouraged, the point comes right at the end. The harvest — the *amazing* harvest. Thirtyfold, sixtyfold, a hundredfold, a harvest of four- to tenfold was considered normal, with a harvest of fifteen times what was sown being exceptionally good. Who was responsible for such a thing? The sower? Of course not. It could be none other than God, it always has been, it always will be. Even when we figure it is all up to us. Fertility facts of the kingdom.

Proper 11
Pentecost 9
Ordinary Time 16
Genesis 28:10-19a

I Am With You

In all of scripture, and even in all of literature, you would be hard pressed to find a character more interesting than Jacob. We meet him first before he is even born — his mother, Rebekah, is in such agony during her pregnancy carrying him and his twin brother that she wants to die. When the babies finally make their appearance, little Esau comes out first, but his brother is holding onto his heel, and, as the legend has it, that is why he was given the name Jacob — it meant "heel" or "trickster" or "supplanter." And since names, then and now, carry baggage, we have a huge clue as to the kind of person this baby is going to become.

Yes, the lad grew up to be a "heel." You remember those stories from your Sunday school lessons. He cheated his brother out of his inheritance. He duped his father, Isaac, on his deathbed. Esau was ready to kill him, but Jacob approached the problem "spatially" — he got out of that space. He ran for the hills, literally. He headed north toward his Uncle Laban in Haran.

Something strange happened then. As Jacob paused on his journey, and with no one hot on his tail, he made camp for the night. His escape had been too hasty to prepare a bedroll, so he just curled up on the ground with a smooth stone for a pillow. Tossing and turning, unable to sleep because of a guilty conscience? Not at all. Like a baby he slept, and dreamed the kind of dream that one would have thought would be reserved for a saint — a ladder reaching from earth to heaven with angels ascending and descending. And standing above it all, the God of all creation saying not, "How dare you?" but, "I am going to bless you. Your descendants will be like the dust of the earth, and you will spread out to the west and to the east, to the north and to the south. All peoples on earth will be blessed through you and your offspring. I am with you and will watch over you wherever you go, and I will bring you back to this land. I will not leave you until I have done what I have promised you."

Wow! I guess we should not be surprised by Jacob's response. He took that stone that he had used for a pillow, propped it up, poured oil on it, and called it *Bethel* ("God's House"), the least expensive sanctuary in the history of religion.

Good ol' Jacob — a scamp and a scallawag, to be sure. But there must have been something redemptive about him because people of faith from generation to generation have heard "I am the God of Abraham, Isaac, and [even] Jacob." Amazing.

The message in this brief story is one of sheer grace. The God who told a scoundrel like Jacob, "I am with you and will watch over you wherever you go," is the same God who speaks to us. When we are frightened by new places, new people, new ideas, new responsibilities, God is there promising, "I am with you." When we feel trapped by problems we cannot solve and stuck with people with whom we cannot get along, God is there promising, "I am with you." When we feel totally alone as Jacob felt out there in the desert, when we feel lost, God is there promising, "I am with you." When we lose hope that anything will ever be better than it is now, when it looks as if evil triumphs and good is trashed, God is there promising, "I am with you!"

Nevertheless

In 1981, Rabbi Harold Kushner wrote *When Bad Things Happen to Good People*, not *Why* Bad Things Happen to Good People. Kushner's point is that bad things *do* happen to good people, and all the time. Terrible accidents like little children being crushed by trucks, young mothers struck down by cancer, innocent victims cruelly destroyed at the hands of terrorists.

Some years ago, a young family died in the crash of their single-engine plane — a father, mother, and their twelve-year-old daughter, Beth, who was one of my son's classmates and who had performed with my daughter in a little theatre group. The two girls had become good friends. Beth was a gorgeous and vivacious child, one of those who would, as the years progressed, be certain to make many a young man's heart flutter (a process which, I am told, had already begun).

My daughter was particularly devastated by the news. She sobbed and sobbed as the terrible truth sank in. It made no sense to her that something like this could occur. In the middle of her pain, she began to feel angry. Sunday school theology had taught her that God rules this world, which meant that God controls all that happens — even plane crashes. As she sat on my lap, she lashed out through her tears in a way that only an eight-year-old can: "God is not very *polite*!"

Later that night, as she lay in her bed and talked with me before saying her prayers, the weeping began again. I tried to explain that even though Beth was no longer here, she was with Jesus —

no crying, no pain, and in a wonderful place. She responded, "God may be happy now, but *I'm not!*"

"No," I replied, "God is not happy. God did not make the plane crash. God does not do things like that. It was a terrible accident, but now God has picked up the pieces and brought Beth and her mommy and daddy home to heaven."

My daughter was not mollified — good theology, but cold comfort. She missed her friend.

A little boy in Sunday school prayed fervently, "Dear God, please bless everybody but my brother, Tommy." The teacher replied that God did indeed understand that little brothers are sometimes hard to live with, but that God *loved* Tommy. "Then he's a mighty funny kind of a God," the little boy said. In our own way and for our own reasons, we might agree. As my daughter expressed it, "God is not very *polite!*"

My son shared with me at the time that one of the class assignments he and Beth had for English was to keep a journal, and one of the reflections was to deal with those things of which they were afraid. Beth had written that she was afraid of dying young. How ironic!

There are too many ironies in this world for my taste. Bad things happen to good people, and I do not like it. Where is God in all this? As a Christian minister, my immediate reaction is to leap to God's defense (as if God needs my help), but some things are hard to explain away.

What are we to make of all this ... of plane crashes, of terrorist attacks, of disasters and miseries? Christians believe that God is in control of this world. God is in charge of everything! So what is going on?

In a way, it may seem like whistling through the graveyard to continue with that affirmation, just as folks try to comfort friends who have just suffered some tragedy that "All things work together for good." Right. Awful things constantly happen ... holocausts, September 11, ethnic cleansings, millions starving in Africa, and so on and so on and so on. Then how can we continue to preach and teach that a sovereign, loving God is in control with any intellectual or philosophical or even theological integrity?

Dr. Albert Winn, pastor, professor, distinguished church leader, answers the question as well as anyone.[1] He notes that at the heart of biblical faith we do not find airtight arguments sealed with a "therefore" — all is right with the world, therefore, let us have faith; therefore, let us praise God. Rather, at the heart of biblical faith we find things that do not logically follow at all, sealed with a "nevertheless." Much is wrong with the world, the mystery of evil is great, *nevertheless* let us have faith, *nevertheless* let us praise God. Perhaps we can better understand the miseries of life if we remember *nevertheless*.

God is sovereign. God is in control. We continue to preach it and teach it. But the question remains: Are we just whistling through the graveyard? Are we like little children, trying to affirm what we know is not true by tightly closing our eyes and trying to make our dream real by endlessly repeating our hope? Is this a great collective self-deception? Not at all.

When I need a reminder, I look at the calendar. I see the first day of the week and I remember what happened one Sunday so many years ago, that first Easter, the day of resurrection. It was that day that guaranteed for time and all eternity that "the wrong shall fail, the right prevail," and that, yes indeed, all things *do* work together for good to those who love God.

---

1. Albert Curry Winn, *A Christian Primer* (Louisville: Westminster/John Knox Press, 1990), pp. 79-80.

Proper 13
Pentecost 11
Ordinary Time 18
Matthew 14:13-21

Bring Them To Me

The early church certainly liked this story — it is the only miracle other than the resurrection that is recorded in all four gospels. At least a zillion sermons have been preached on it — sermons about miracles in general, sermons about Jesus' remarkable appeal as crowds traipsed around the countryside after him, sermons about Jesus' compassion, sermons about our role in God's work — Jesus gave the food to the disciples who then distributed it to the crowd ("Go, thou, and do likewise."). The always reliable focus on the generosity and unselfishness of that one little boy of whom we read in John's account of the event (John 6:1-13). There are any number of sermons here.

The disciples had come back to Jesus after their mission to the countryside. Two by two they had gone out, preaching and healing. Now they have returned for a debriefing retreat, telling Jesus about successes and failures, sorrows and joys. And it is at this moment, we hear the story of the miraculous meal. Why? Why here? Why now? I think the answer is one that will speak to any of us when we are concerned that what we bring to a particular task may be inadequate.

Listen again to the disciples: "This is a remote place, and it's already getting late. Send the crowds away, so they can go to the villages and buy themselves some food."

Jesus says, "Naw, they can stay; *you* feed them."

"What? We have here only five loaves of bread and two fish, and that is not enough!"

Lord, only five loaves of bread and two fish. Lord, only five loaves of bread and two fish. That is the response of the ages when people feel overwhelmed by the task confronting them.

We all feel that way at times. The parents worried about guiding the children on the right path despite all the pressures to stray. "What are we to do? We have only five loaves of bread and two fish." The laid-off worker who struggles to survive in a difficult economy. "I have only five loaves of bread and two fish." The spouse who is desperately trying to make a go of a troubled marriage, but knowing nowhere to turn to rekindle the passion. "I have only five loaves of bread and two fish."

Certainly that was the response of the disciples when the crowds followed them on their retreat with Jesus. Jesus says, "You give them something to eat."

What? We only have five loaves of bread and two fish.

Fortunately for the twelve, and for us, Jesus intervenes. He says softly, "Bring them here to me ... and looking up to heaven, he gave thanks and broke the loaves. Then he gave them to the disciples, and the disciples gave them to the people. They all ate and were satisfied, and the disciples picked up twelve basketfuls of broken pieces that were left over."

There is the good news for anyone feeling inadequate in the face of the pressures of life. The answer is, "No, we often do not have what it takes." At best, in the face of overwhelming odds, we only have five loaves of bread and two fish. But we have a friend who whispers, "Bring them to me."

Remember this the next time you encounter a moment when life seems so big and you feel so small, heading off into the dreary desert of the day-to-day. Remember, someone is close who can do what you and I cannot, someone who can take our paltry little handful of loaves and fish and turn them into a feast. Again, Jesus whispers, "Bring them to me," and suddenly, miraculously even, our little becomes a lot.

Proper 14
Pentecost 12
Ordinary Time 19
Matthew 14:22-33

Little Faith

If the gospel writer had not identified Peter as the one who wanted to walk on the water, we probably could have figured it out. After all, Peter was always the impetuous one, the one to leap before he looked. True, he occasionally made a fool of himself, as he did on this occasion, but no one could ever doubt the depth of his commitment and love for Jesus. When it comes right down to it, Peter was a man of incredible faith. Of all those in the boat, he was the only one who had enough confidence in his Lord to think that, simply at Jesus' say-so, a man could walk on water. That is faith!

Jesus said, "Come." So, as the record has it, Peter got out of the boat and walked on the water ... for a step or two anyway. Suddenly that big fisherman began to think about what he was doing, about the wind and waves that were lashing all around him, about the fact that men do not walk on water, and he began to go down like a rock. "Lord, save me!"

Jesus responded, of course. He rescued the sinking sailor, gently chided him for his "little faith," and brought him back to the boat. Great old story! Of course, we have heard it since our earliest days in Sunday school, so perhaps it has become routine in the telling. We even joke about it.

There is one that has gone around for years about three ministers out fishing together in a small boat. One of them, suddenly realizing that he had left his tackle box in the cabin, stepped out of the boat, and walked on the water over to shore. Just then, the second one said he had forgotten his faithful fishing hat on the front seat of the car. He, too, stepped out of the boat and walked on the water over to shore. When they had both returned, the third minister who had watched this remarkable demonstration with mouth open and eyes wide, reasoned to himself, "My faith is as strong as theirs. I can do that, too." So he stepped out of the boat and promptly sank to the bottom. His two companions dragged him out, but once they got him in the boat, he was determined not to be shown up. He stepped out once more, and immediately sank again. As his friends pulled him out, he sputtered, "My faith is as strong as yours. Why can't I walk on the water?"

The first two looked at each another and one finally said, "We'd better tell him where those rocks are before he drowns himself." Ah, ha.

To be sure, the Bible story was never intended as a joke. We did not learn it that way and do not think of it that way now. We hear how great Jesus is to be able to perform such a miracle as water-walking. We hear how foolish Peter was to take his eyes off Jesus; to waver in his faith. Then we challenge ourselves never to lose sight of the Lord if we hope to survive the winds and waves of life.

> *Turn your eyes upon Jesus;*
> *Look full in His wonderful face;*
> *And the things of earth will grow strangely dim,*
> *In the light of His glory and grace.*
> — Helen H. Lemmel, 1922

And not only that, you will be able to walk on water. Sure! Do you believe that? I don't. And, honestly, I do not ever want to, because that kind of faith almost always ends up as a big disappointment. It ends up sinking like Peter and that preacher.

Do you remember what Jesus said to that big fisherman as he was rescuing him? He said, "You of little faith." We might "Tut-Tut" about that and say he should have trusted completely. But note that Jesus did not say, "You of *no* faith." We have already agreed that Peter had more faith than anyone else in the boat. But Jesus called it *little* faith.

Maybe faith is like knowledge — a little of it is a dangerous thing. A little faith that is confounded by overblown expectations might lead us, like it did Peter, down a very slippery slope. It might lead us to presume that God will act in a certain way just because we want God to, and often without any effort of our own.

We pray for healing, and then do not take the medicine. We pray for our children, but do not teach them values. We pray for a good marriage, but do not talk to one another. We pray for peace, but do not work for justice. We pray for the homeless, but do not provide shelter. We pray for the unemployed, but do not offer jobs or training. No wonder we are finally reduced to crying, "Lord, save me!"

I read somewhere of an itinerant evangelist who looked for any opportunity he could find to do his preaching. One day he saw a crowd gathered in a public park, so he climbed up on a tree stump and began to share the gospel. Not far away, another fellow heard what was going on and, mocking the preacher, began challenging God, if there *was* a God, to knock him down. On and on he went in a voice of derision. Finally, the preacher climbed down from his makeshift pulpit, walked over to the challenger, and *blam* ... he knocked that sucker flat. The stunned crowd just stood in wide-eyed silence. Slowly, the preacher turned around to them and quietly said, "I never expect God to do what I can do myself." Good thinking.

The lesson in all this is that faith in a living, loving Lord is not the same as believing in magic. Christian faith is firm in the conviction that God can do anything God wants to do, even tricks like walking on water if such be the choice. But those are not the norm, and frankly, they are cold comfort when we are faced with real-life winds and waves that are the norm: the loss of a loved one, the pain of a family crisis, even the prospect of our own death. In those moments, those times when we want to shout for help, Mr. or Ms. Little-faith cries out for Jesus to rescue. But Mr. or Ms. Real-faith is content simply with knowing that Jesus is *there*, and in his unfailing love, able to sustain us even through the most violent storm. Once we get to that point, with the disciples in the boat after their wet friend had been brought back, we can declare to Jesus, "You are not Merlin or Blackstone or David Copperfield. You are far more. Truly, you are the Son of God."

Proper 15
Pentecost 13
Ordinary Time 20
Genesis 45:1-15

Payback Time

If there was ever anyone who had an excuse to look for re-venge, it was Joseph. As you recall from your earliest Sunday school days, young Joey was his father's favorite son, a bitter enough pill for his brothers to swallow, but the boy did everything he could to rub their faces in it, and the result was that his fed-up siblings took matters into their own hands and sold him into slavery. (And you thought *you* had a dysfunctional family!)

The Midianites who bought the boy were on their way to Egypt where they would soon sell Joseph once more, this time to a man named Potiphar, the head of pharaoh's security force. Joseph did well, under the circumstances, eventually being placed in charge of Potiphar's entire household, an incredible honor for a slave. But Potiphar's wife had her own ideas about honor — she tried to se-duce the young man, and when he refused her advances, she yelled, "Rape!"

Joseph was in jail, once again the victim. But here again, he prospered, gaining the respect of fellow prisoners and guards. Even-tually two of pharaoh's servants found themselves behind the same bars where they all became friends. This was a scenario that (after a few dream interpretations) eventually led to Joseph's release.

To make a long story short, pharaoh had an eye for talent and made our Hebrew hero the prime minister of Egypt — from the jail house to the penthouse. Not bad for a bratty kid who had been sold into slavery by his brothers!

A famine settled on the near East. Jacob told his sons to go to Egypt to buy some grain. They did, and in the process they met

Joseph — only they did not know it was Joseph. It happens twice. Finally, Joseph revealed his true identity. The brothers were shocked and rightly scared — payback time! But Joseph did not do that. In fact, he stunned them with these words:

> *Do not be distressed and do not be angry with your-*
> *selves for selling me here, because it was to save lives*
> *that God sent me ahead of you. For two years now there*
> *has been famine in the land, and for the next five years*
> *there will not be plowing and reaping. But God sent me*
> *ahead of you to preserve for you a remnant on earth*
> *and to save your lives by a great deliverance. So then,*
> *it was not you who sent me here, but God.*

The story goes on. The brothers went back to Canaan and told their aged father that Joseph was still alive. He could not believe it, but eventually they convince him to go to Egypt with them. He made the trip and was reunited with the son he had given up for dead so many years before. Then he met the pharaoh who offered to let Joseph's family settle in for as long as they like. The family moved to Egypt and lived in peace there for many years. Finally, Jacob died at the ripe old age of 147.

Then it was just Joseph and his brothers. Again they feared payback time — with Jacob gone, brother Joe would be free to take his revenge. So they told Joseph, "Oh, by the way, before Dad died he told us to tell you to treat us kindly."

Listen to Joseph's gracious response: "Don't be afraid. Am I in the place of God? You intended to harm me, but God intended it for good to accomplish what is now being done, the saving of many lives. So then, don't be afraid. I will provide for you and your children." And he reassured them and spoke kindly to them (Genesis 50:20-21).

The world could use a few more Josephs, couldn't it? It is pretty mean out there, and people can be incredible.

Someone has suggested that sermons from Christian pulpits about forgiveness should include some instruction as to how to go about it. That is a good idea. Here are some points from the literature of one of the twelve-step programs:

1. Write down in black and white the reasons why we are angry with (someone). Writing clarifies emotions that have been confused and buried in us, sometimes for years. Also by setting down our grievances in black and white, we place a boundary around them. Our grievances are only so big and no bigger. The hurt had a beginning and it can have an end.

2. Consider "giving away" (telling) what we have written to some trusted person. Consider symbolically releasing the hurt, such as by burning or tearing up the paper.

3. Pray. Pray for willingness to forgive, and pray for the person who has wronged us, daily, asking God to bless them with good things we want for ourselves. If we keep praying for them faithfully, sooner or later our feelings will change. When our feelings change, when we find ourselves being sincere in asking God to bless our former enemies, then we will know we have forgiven them.

Payback time. As a flesh-and-blood victim of a horrible crime, Joseph had all the reason in the world to look for his chance. But there is a better way. Joseph knew it. And we know it.

Proper 16
Pentecost 14
Ordinary Time 21
Matthew 16:13-20

Who Do You Say That I Am?

Many years ago, in my seminary days, our first course in Systematic Theology dealt with basically the same question as that which the Lord posed to his disciples. Our professor described Jesus as "the proleptic, salvific, hidden appearance of the eschatological kingdom of God." On our way out of class that morning, we chuckled at the whole thing:

> *Jesus said to them, "Who do* you *say that I am?"*
> *Simon Peter replied, "You are the proleptic, salvific, hidden appearance of the eschatological kingdom of God."*
> *Jesus answered and said unto him, "What?"*

The definitions of theology professors notwithstanding, one would think that after almost 2,000 years, the question of who or what is Jesus, the ultimate question, would have been settled, at least for Christians. But such is apparently not the case, and that is why we have regular controversies about books and films "starring" Jesus. Faithful people yell foul and call for boycotts, protests, and the like, but I personally am glad for anything that gets people to look at Jesus again, because looking at Jesus is something Christians do not do enough.

Several factors play into that. First, our theological formulations about the person and work of Jesus Christ were fairly well settled for us by the church fathers in the early centuries of the faith. We repeat the words of the Nicene Creed:

... one Lord Jesus Christ, the only begotten Son of God
... God of God, Light of Light, Very God of Very God;
Begotten, not made ... one substance with the Father ...
incarnate by the Holy Ghost of the Virgin Mary, and
was made man ...

We remember the words of the *Shorter Catechism*: "God and man, in two distinct natures, and one Person forever." We believe all that even if we do not understand it any more than the "proleptic, salvific, hidden appearance of the eschatological kingdom of God." The theology is settled for us! "You are the Christ, the Son of the living God."

A second reason for not looking much at Jesus is that, for the most part, our picture of him is well established. We are content with the mental images of Christ we have had since childhood: a beautiful baby in an ethereally lighted antiseptic manger; a white-robed teacher gently and lovingly instructing attentive crowds on lush, green hillsides; a brilliant and insightful debater who calmly and courteously skewers opponents with his incontrovertible logic; an unfortunate martyr who died with supreme dignity. This is our picture. Yes, we want to say more than the ancient gossip about his being another John the Baptist or Elijah or Jeremiah or some other prophet. But those childish images are generally sufficient, even if they end up giving us a hothouse flower kind of Lord. This is what we most often mean with "You are the Christ, the Son of the living God."

A third reason for not looking too closely at Jesus is that we would simply rather not. Our pat theological answers and our warm mental images are just fine, thank you. We have enough challenges in our lives. Our children are a challenge, making ends meet is a challenge, staying healthy is a challenge, the environment is a challenge. We do not need that from our religion, too! Please, let us have *something* in this life that is not a challenge, something we can count on, something we do not have to worry about.

To be sure, there are parts of the biblical picture of Christ that absolutely challenge us — we would rather not notice Jesus' evident bias in favor of the poor and marginalized of society; as wealthy Americans we would rather he not remind us, "It is easier for a camel to go through the eye of a needle than for a rich man to enter the kingdom of heaven." As good church goers, we would rather not notice that the ones for whom Jesus had the most contempt were the religious folk of his day; for people who want comfort rather than challenge from their faith, we surely do not want to hear, "If any want to become my followers, let them deny themselves and take up their cross." Those are all a part of the biblical picture, but "No, Lord. Let us simply say, 'You are the Christ, the Son of the living God,' and leave it at that."

G. K. Chesterton once remarked, "The only way to make a good statue is to throw away good marble." We might or might not agree with what is "chipped away" in these books and films about Jesus, but that is all right. If they challenge people to actually *think* about Jesus, to see and hear him in a new way, it accomplishes more than most of the traditional images ever do.

Can we then learn from it, even though some of it might be questionable? Of course. During my doctoral studies, one of my professors recounted an experience from his early days in seminary. He had gone out to a small country church for worship one Sunday and was mortified to hear some of the worst theology he had ever encountered coming from a Presbyterian pulpit. As he sat and listened and heard this wrong, that wrong, and the other wrong, he began to wonder how in the world God could ever use this kind of drivel. Then he realized that God had indeed used it; God had spoken to him that morning by forcing him to reflect on his faith. The result: He got something out of it. He might not have gotten what the preacher had intended, but God did speak.

Millions upon millions of words have been written and spoken about Jesus. As Emerson once noted, "The name of Jesus is not so much written as ploughed into the history of the world." But none of those words have ever been able to tell the whole story. As that great preacher of the nineteenth century, Horace Bushnell, once said, "Who can satisfy himself with anything he can say concerning Jesus Christ?"

"Who do you say that I am?" asks Jesus. Proleptic? Salvific? Eschatological? Or anything like that? I doubt it. No. With Simon Peter, the answer is, "You are the Christ, the Son of the living God."

Proper 17
Pentecost 15
Ordinary Time 22
Exodus 3:1-15

The Bush Is Still Burning

The burning bush, or more correctly, the *un*burning bush. It was probably an ordinary bramble bush, the most usual kind of vegetation in those parts. The fire would not have been that remarkable because spontaneous combustion is not unheard of in dry, hot, desert country. But a fire that burns but does not consume? Moses came over to investigate. Suddenly, he heard his name: "Moses, Moses!" The voice was coming from the bush.

Moses leaned in, his head cocked to one side in wonder. "Here I am."

The voice again. "Do not come any closer! Take off your sandals, for the place on which you are standing is holy ground."

"Huh?" Moses, looking as bewildered as you or I might be, fumbled around with the thongs that held his sandals in place, removed them, then looked quizzically at the bush again.

The voice spoke. "I am the God of your father, the God of Abraham, the God of Isaac, and the God of Jacob."

Right. This is one of those passages that Bill Cosby could have a field day with. The bush spoke ... the voice of God! Right. Am I on *Candid Camera*? Lucky for us, no cameras back then. Moses responded by shielding his face, because he knew to look at God was to die.

God says, "I have indeed seen the misery of my people in Egypt. I have heard them crying out because of their slave drivers, and I am concerned about their suffering. So I have come down to rescue them from the hand of the Egyptians and to bring them up out of that land into a good and spacious land, a land flowing with

144

milk and honey...." This is all well and good. One wonders why it took God so long to notice, considering it had only been 400 years that the people have been enslaved, but that is another story. The present problem is God's choice of a leader — this eighty-year-old shepherd whose only entry to the corridors of Egyptian power would be through a justice system (such as it is) that only knows him as a fugitive from a murder charge.

As might be expected, Moses demurs. "Who am I that I should go to the pharaoh, and bring the Israelites out of Egypt?" Good question. We can all agree that God's choices are not always easily explained.

Note something — God never defends the decision, never explains why the choice. In answer to Moses' "Who am I?" objection, the response was simply, "I will be with you." Moses was right — "Who *was* he?" Nobody. No matter. "I will be with you." And that is what ultimately counts. I love the "sign" that God promised: "And this will be the sign to you that it is I who have sent you: When you have brought the people out of Egypt, you will worship God on this mountain." In other words, the only sign you will see is in the rearview mirror, hindsight. One day, when you are back here on this mountain and worshiping with your Hebrew brothers and sisters, you will think back to this moment and realize that God was with you all along, just as promised.

"That is all well and good, God," Moses continued, "but what happens when I get to Egypt and tell the people, 'The God of your ancestors has sent me to you'? They are gonna look at me like I am nuts! And who could blame them? What am I gonna tell them if they ask *which* god has sent me, what shall I say?"

Here is where the rubber meets the road. God's response has gotten more theological ink over the years than anyone would care to calculate. *Which* god? "God said to Moses, 'I AM WHO I AM. This is what you are to say to the Israelites: I AM has sent me to you.'" What could that mean?

A quick and dirty language lesson here: Apparently early on, someone somewhere noted the similarity of the four consonants of the Hebrew name for God (transliterated), Y H W H, and the three consonants of the verb "to be," H Y H. So saying, be aware that

Hebrew does not use this verb as a common coupler the way English does. Where we would ask, "What is your name?" Hebrew would ask, "What your name?" Hebrew reserves H Y H for much more significant meanings. So we translate this passage, "I am who I am," or even "I will be who I will be." This is the God who *is*, the God who really *exists* (as opposed to those false gods we worship who are no gods at all). Even more, this is the God who is present, especially at those moments of deepest need. This is the God with no limits, the God who will be whatever is necessary, no matter what the situation. In another time and place, Isaiah expressed the name as *Immanuel*, "God with us," the name made even more real to you and me in the coming of Jesus.

Of course, by the time of Christ, this divine name had taken on a mystique of its own. In fact, the religious establishment was ready to stone Jesus as a blasphemer for using the special name in reference to himself (John 8:56-59).

For what it is worth, the establishment was at least partly right — no, Jesus was not a blasphemer — yes, he did use the divine name in a personal way. Over and over and over again, in fact. And over and over and over, we find it offers a wonderful word of comfort.

Think of some of the things Jesus said, and then relate them to your own life.

- For you who are hungry for spiritual nourishment that has been neglected in the too-fast pace of modern life, the bush is still burning. Jesus says, "I AM the bread of life" (John 6:35).
- To you who have strayed from the straight and narrow path and now want to find your way back, the bush is still burning. Jesus says, "I AM the light of the world" (John 8:12).
- To you who feel that you cannot get back to the path because you have strayed so far, the bush is still burning. Jesus says, "I AM the good shepherd" (John 10:11).
- To you who have been drained of any joy in life by depression, despair, and grief, the bush is still burning. Jesus says, "I AM the vine" (John 15:5).

- To you teenagers who want solid guidance in your life choices — school, career, mate — the bush is still burning. Jesus says, "I AM the way" (John 14:6).
- To you who are wrestling with the ethical puzzles of a confused and confusing world not sure what is right or wrong anymore, the bush is still burning. Jesus says, "I AM the truth" (John 14:6).
- To you who are coming near the end of this earthly journey and wonder what lies ahead, the bush is still burning. Jesus says, "I AM the resurrection and the life" (John 11:35).

Carefully scan the mountainsides of your life. Be alert. Listen quietly. Perhaps a verse of scripture, a word of prayer, a moment of fellowship, a line from a lesson, a sentence from a sermon, the touch of a hand, or the warmth of a smile. That voice. Speaking to you. The bush is still burning.

Proper 18
Pentecost 16
Ordinary Time 23
Exodus 12:1-14

Remembering 9/11

"This is a day you are to commemorate; for the generations to come you shall celebrate it as a festival to the Lord — a lasting ordinance," or as the King James has it, "You shall observe it as an ordinance forever." The establishment of the Passover, one of the most important of all Jewish festivals. And they have observed it forever. Every year since, and down to our own day, Jewish families have gathered at the traditional *Seder* meal. The patriarch of the household asks the children, "What makes this night different than all other nights?" The youngsters respond with the Exodus story of God's miraculous deliverance of their people. Some things are important to remember.

We understand that. I wonder if in any American home on September 11 anyone will ask, "What makes this day different from all other days?" We know why someone might.

September 11 was a horrible day. Most of us can recall exactly where we were and what we were doing when we heard. We were glued to whatever television sets were handy. I have no idea how many times we saw the second plane fly into the south tower, or how many times we saw them collapse. Gracious, plenty; too many for lots of people.

Our national response was, for the most part, wonderful. We saw true heroism in the work of New York's police and firefighters. I doubt that any of us not directly related had given much thought to the life-threatening danger these public servants lived with day in and day out until that day. On September 11 we saw their courage and dedication, and it was a marvel to behold.

As the perpetrators were identified, we quickly put things into perspective. Yes, there were a few isolated incidents of hate crimes committed against people who appeared to be from the Middle East, but, for the most part, people understood that these horrific acts had been the work of a fanatical fringe — to tar all of Islam with the brush of Al-Qaeda would be the same as tarring all Christianity with the brush of the Ku Klux Klan. We reacted better than that.

There was a wonderful outpouring of support for the victims and their families. Remember the long lines at the blood banks? The billions of dollars ungrudgingly given to charities who would provide assistance, in some cases more money than they knew what to do with? Americans are a generous people. We already knew that. And not only generous to our own; we are generous with the whole world. That is why the questions came later that day: "Why would they do such a thing? Why do they hate us so?"

One of the pleasant surprises of 9/11 was the flood of sympathy from around the world. Remember? Even nations we would normally not think of as friends stood in solidarity with us and condemned the attacks. The footage shown on television of some young Palestinians celebrating the news was played over and over again, and as it was, we began to notice that folks in the background were not celebrating at all. It turned out that there was far more footage of people around the globe reacting with shock and horror strained through tears.

As the day wore on, the numbness we had felt at the first word of the attacks began to wear off. The tragedy was touching us at the very depths of our being. We heard the reports of phone conversations from the upper floors of the Trade Center towers, or the cell phone calls from United flight 93, not to express fear or anger, but simply to say, "I'm stuck up here; I don't think I'm gonna make it ... I love you ... Take care of the children." We wanted to talk with our own families. We appreciated in a new way how fragile life really is.

No doubt that is why church attendance took such a jump in the days following the tragedy. Even people who, for every other day of their lives were blissfully irreligious suddenly found themselves in church ... prayer services that night, memorial services on the Friday following, Sunday worship.

Suddenly we heard again the words of our lesson. God's instruction to Israel about another important day: "This is a day you are to commemorate; for the generations to come you shall celebrate it as a festival to the Lord — a lasting ordinance." Why? To insure that the nation remembers who it is and *whose* it is.

Remembering 9/11 can help us do the same. We remember we are Americans, but we also remember we are Christians, and that says something about how to respond to attacks:

- We are Christians who remember the word of the Lord that says "Vengeance is mine, I will repay" (Romans 12:19).
- We are Christians who remember the word of the Lord that says, "If your enemy is hungry, feed him; if he is thirsty, give him something to drink" (Romans 12:20).
- We are Christians who remember the word of the Lord that says, "Do not be overcome by evil, but overcome evil with good" (Romans 12:21).
- We are Christians who remember the word of the Lord that says, "Love your enemies and pray for those who persecute you" (Matthew 5:44).

Remembering 9/11. It will be painful. But, by the grace of God, it will be helpful.

Proper 19
Pentecost 17
Ordinary Time 24
Matthew 18:21-35

The Power To Change The Past

A fellow went to the hospital to visit his partner who had been taken strangely ill and was near death. Suddenly, the dying man began to speak. "John," he said, "before I go I have to confess some things and get your forgiveness. I want you to know that I robbed the firm of $100,000 several years ago. I sold our secret formula to our competition, and John, I am the one who supplied your wife with the evidence that got her the divorce and cost you a small fortune. Will you forgive me?"

John murmured, "That's okay, old man. I am the one who gave you the poison." Seventy times seven.

In a perverse and extreme way, the partner reflects modern attitudes toward forgiveness. We live in a balance-sheet world that demands justice. Society counsels, "Don't get mad; get even." When things do not go our way, we are advised to "Sue their socks off!" Despite growing up with advice like "Forgive and forget" or being reminded that "To err is human, to forgive divine" and our regular "Forgive us our debts as we forgive our debtors," we do not find much forgiveness out there. Children cannot forgive their parents and parents cannot forgive their children. I know wives who cannot forgive their husbands and husbands who cannot forgive their wives. Arabs have difficulty forgiving Jews; and Jews, Arabs. There is not much forgiveness anywhere.

That is nothing new though. Two-thousand years ago, the question was posed, "Lord, how often am I to forgive ... seven times?" Peter's question to Jesus was a good one (and his offer more than generous — after all, if someone wrongs you over and over and over again, you will be inclined to call time out before the seventh go-round). It was rabbinic teaching that a man must forgive his brother three times. No doubt Peter thought that he was being incredibly charitable, for he takes the rabbinic teaching, doubles it, adds one for good measure, and suggests (with eager self-satisfaction, no doubt) that it will be enough if he forgives seven times. Peter thought he would be warmly commended, I suspect, but Jesus' answer was that the Christian must forgive, depending on your translation 77 times or seventy times seven. 490? But this is celestial arithmetic. Jesus meant $70 \times 7 \times 77 \times 70 \times 7 \times 77$ — on to infinity — forgiveness with no limit at all.

The Lord then told the story of the servant forgiven a humongous debt who went out and dealt mercilessly with a fellow servant who owed him a tiny bit — 1/600,000th of the original amount. No forgiveness here — debtors' prison. The king heard about what happened, called the servant in and had him imprisoned because he was not willing to show the same forgiveness he himself had been shown. Jesus' conclusion was, "So my heavenly Father will also do to everyone of you, if you do not forgive your brother or sister from your heart." Scary.

There are several places in scripture that indicate a quid pro quo concerning forgiveness — if we don't give it, we won't get it. I know the Lord would not intend for us to build a theology on that emphasis — too much else in the Bible makes plain that God's forgiveness of our sin comes because of what Christ did, not on what we do or fail to do. But the harshness of the story's ending has its inescapable truth — the one who fails to forgive ends up in a prison of his own making, now unable to experience forgiveness for himself.

Forgiveness is a decision about how to deal with what supposedly is beyond our reach — history. One choice we can make about wrongs we have suffered is to seek revenge: poison your partner ... "Don't get mad, get even" ... "Sue their socks off." The idea behind those options is misconceived justice, that there is a balance owed to you, and somehow you will make the wrongdoer pay. To choose forgiveness is to give up that balance-sheet view. By letting go of our sense of being wronged, we can also let go of bitterness and resentment and open ourselves to much more healthy and wholesome emotions.

Real forgiveness is *not* a little thing — in fact, it is one of the most powerful forces in the universe. It is the only thing in this world that actually has the power to change the past.

Proper 20
Pentecost 18
Ordinary Time 25
Philippians 1:21-30

To Die Is Gain

"For me to live is Christ and to die is gain." So says the apostle Paul. Really? We are tempted to mutter, "Not for us, it isn't." We look around the world and see little children dying of exposure and starvation and our hearts are torn because so little is being done. We watch in horror as older citizens waste away in the relentless onslaught of age finally wanting nothing so much as surrender. We see friends knocked down in the prime of life by debilitating disease that finally claims them, and we hate death! Instead of seeing death as sweet release, we think of ourselves and feel a profound emptiness, a deep sense of loss. Loss is the opposite of gain, at least for those of us who are left behind. Think of death as Paul did? Not easy.

Why? Selfishness, obviously. We would much rather not be deserted by our loved ones. My dad has been gone from me for years; I would love to be able to talk with him again about things of mutual concern. I would like to share church experiences, to talk of preaching and teaching, to ask advice ... maybe even to play a little golf. I wish he were here. I know his life today is better by far than anything he ever experienced on this earth (especially the way he played golf), but selfishly, I can still wish he were here.

But there is more. Our thoughts about death, our dislike of it, respond to some innate reverence for physical life. We grow up learning that all life is precious. In backyards all over the world there are buried shoe boxes with the remains of pet turtles and parakeets over which children have shed sad tears. Young soldiers return from the horrors of war with reports of nothing so awful than coming face to face with another young soldier from the other side whom they are forced to kill. The abortion debates that continue in our nation center on this belief in the sanctity of life. There is something about life that we see as grand and glorious, which makes its end so utterly depressing.

Perhaps death distresses us so because we see what it does to those who are still here: family and friends. We feel it. On the night my father died, after all the friends and acquaintances had come and gone, the family sat around the kitchen table talking quietly. We talked about our dad. We missed him. We were not worried about him. With every fiber of our collective being we knew where he was and that he could triumphantly say with Paul, "for me ... to die is gain." But finally Mom said, "I've lost my best friend." It was a heartrending moment.

Tennyson wrote:

In Memoriam
That loss is common would not make
My own less bitter, rather more.
Too common! Never morning wore to evening
But some heart did break.

That is what we hate about death ... what it does to those who are left behind.

Then can we ever get to the place of thinking about death as the apostle Paul did? He said, "I desire to depart and be with Christ, which is better by far." The Greek word he uses is the word for striking camp, loosening the tent ropes, pulling up the tent pins, and moving on. Death is a moving on.

As to what awaits following the move, we have only the sketchiest details, but we firmly believe that there is more to life than what we experience here. We believe that death is not a period but a comma in the story of life, and we know what Jesus said: "In my Father's house there are many dwelling places. If it were not so, would I have told you that I go to prepare a place for you? And if I go and prepare a place for you, I will come again and will take you to myself, so that where I am, there you may be also" (John 14:2-3). No wonder Paul says, "to die is gain." He has a place in heaven set aside for him and his landlord is Jesus Christ.

As to not knowing what lies on the other side, we know what scripture has to say about it, of course ... gates of pearl, streets of gold, bejeweled walls ... poetic language to describe something indescribable. No more pain, no more tears, no more death. It will be incredible. The wonderful evangelist of a previous generation, Dwight. L. Moody said, "Someday you will read in the paper that D. L. Moody of East Northfield, Massachusetts, is dead. Don't believe a word of it! At that moment I shall be more alive than I am now. I shall have gone up higher, that's all ... out of this old clay tenement into a house that is immortal, a body that death cannot touch, that sin cannot taint, a body fashioned like unto his glorious body."

It was the same kind of confidence that enabled Dietrich Bonhoeffer to say, as Nazi soldiers led him to his execution, "For me this is the beginning of a new life, eternal life." Moody and Bonhoeffer were right, of course. For them, to die was gain.

Years ago, a clergyman was summoned to the deathbed of an old man in one of the slums of London. Flight after flight of stairs he mounted until he came to the topmost flat and found his way into a miserable room with hardly any furniture. There a poor half-starved old soul lay in great pain. As the minister came into the room, he could not help but say, "Oh, but I am sorry for you."

"Sorry for me?" the old man replied. "Why, think of my prospects." Indeed.

"For me, to live is Christ and to die is gain."

Salvation

... continue to work out your salvation with fear and trembling for it is God who works in you to will and to act according to his good purpose.
— Philippians 1:12-13

Wait a minute, Paul. In Sunday school we learned we are saved by *grace* through our faith in Jesus. Salvation is a free gift. We learned that Jesus saves, we don't save ourselves! "Are you saved?" is still the question of the television preachers and tent-meeting evangelists. Salvation.

Truth be told, most folks associate the word salvation with going to heaven — "Pie in the sky when you die." As we have noted earlier, the word comes from a Latin root, *salus,* that has nothing specifically to do with life after death. It means "health" or "wholeness," very similar in meaning to the Hebrew word *shalom* that people over-simplify in translation as "peace," because it, too, carries the idea of wholeness.

The ultimate concern of the Bible, from Genesis to Revelation, is salvation. Look back to the story of creation. In the beginning everything was good. But Adam and Eve sinned — they ate the forbidden fruit from the Tree of the Knowledge of Good and Evil. They decided to think for themselves — no God was needed to separate right from wrong, order from chaos, provide wholeness ... salvation. But they were mistaken. This was the way Israelite mothers and fathers explained to their children why so much was wrong with the world. Human arrogance upset God's good order,

157

and the Genghis Kahns and Hitlers and Sadaam Husseins of this world have offered stark and tragic testimony to that ever since.

But the ancient Hebrews believed more. They knew that God would not leave the world in disarray, nor would God leave the covenant people to fend for themselves. When the psalmist declares, "The Lord is my strength and my song; he has become my salvation" (Psalm 118:14), it is an affirmation that God delivers the people from all sorts of disasters — slavery in Egypt, wars with the Canaanites, bondage in Babylon. Indeed, one of the great heroes of ancient Israel, the one who led the people into the promised land, was named *Yeshua*, Joshua, the Hebrew word for salvation. There is little or no concern with life after death in the Old Testament. Salvation is here-and-now, protection from enemies, a restoration of order.

By the time we get to the New Testament, we find another powerful personality named "Salvation" ... *Yeshua*, which Greek turns into *Iesus* ... Jesus. In the announcement of his coming, the angel told Joseph, "You shall call his name Jesus, for he shall save his people from their sins" (Matthew 1:21). Indeed, there were all sorts of little boys being born around the time of Christ whose Jewish moms and dads named them Jesus in the hope that their son would be the promised Messiah, the Deliverer, the salvation of Israel from the bondage of Rome, the one who would restore God's good order. Life after death was still no issue.

As Jesus began his ministry, something new became apparent. The salvation he was offering was much more than political deliverance for the chosen people. He said that he had come "to preach good news to the poor ... proclaim release to the captives ... [restore] sight to the blind ..." (Luke 4:18), "to seek and to save the lost" (Luke 19:10). To the woman he healed of a hemorrhage, the blind man who could now see, the leper who had been cleansed, he said, "Your faith has saved you." Salvation was not a promise of pie in the sky, by and by, but a restoration of order in the here and now.

By the time we come to the end of the Bible, the book of Revelation, we find more clearly than anywhere else that salvation, restoring order, goes beyond this life. In its complicated but beautifully poetic way, Revelation affirms to the early church, people who were in danger for their very lives because of their commitment to Christ, that God will deliver, will save God's people and will make creation good again: no more hunger, no more thirst, no more tears, no more death. Salvation.

The Christian message is that God's plan *is* salvation. As the gospel writer has it, "For God sent not his Son into the world to condemn the world, but that the world through him might be saved" (John 3:17). Salvation is something much more than a promise of "pie in the sky, by and by." It is nothing less than making a sick creation healthy and whole again. Even here and now. And as Paul would insist, we even have a hand in it.

Proper 22
Pentecost 20
Ordinary Time 27
Exodus 20:1-4, 7-9, 12-20

God Cares About Justice

God cares about justice! Hardly a startling statement. That has been a bedrock principle of religion for centuries. For some folks, that is God's most important attribute — if you get out of line, God's gonna get you! Justice, after all. In fact, it is precisely that kind of thinking that gives some dear hearts great comfort — an assurance that, one day, God will make everything right: "the wrong shall fail / the right prevail," the upside down will be made right side up, the good will be rewarded and the evil will pay.

We find evidence of God's concern early on in the pages of scripture in the divine dealings with the covenant community of Israel. The most prominent statement on God's set of standards for justice is the Ten Commandments.

The Decalogue is often misunderstood, and particularly as it has been caught up in the "culture wars" of recent years. Most notoriously, Alabama Judge Roy Moore was sued by the American Civil Liberties Union and the Alabama Free Thought Association for displaying the Ten Commandments on his courtroom wall. Judge Moore's contention was that these rules formed the basis of western jurisprudence and they would be a good reminder of where we have all come from. Moore lost that case, but used the fallout to mount a campaign for the State Supreme Court, a race that he won which eventually led him to the lofty position of Chief Justice. From that perch, he decided to up the ante by, instead of simply posting the commandments on the wall, having them engraved on a two-and-a-half ton hunk of granite, then late one night, installing it in the courthouse rotunda. Another legal challenge ensued, and this time, the judge not only lost the case, he lost his job.

A good deal of misunderstanding has burdened the interpretation of the Decalogue. These are not laws — they have no penalties attached for breaking them. In the Hebrew Bible, they are known simply as the Ten Words, God's words for the establishment of the kind of society in which we would all like to live.

It would be wonderful to say that our twenty-first-century society has taken them seriously and tried, as Judge Moore in his rather unusual way did, to use them as the basis for our life together. Sadly, we know such is not the case. In fact, it is *so* not the case that we have every right to be angry, the righteous indignation that Jesus himself felt when he saw things that ought not to be.

- We can be angry that a nation that prides itself on providing "equal justice under law" provides it depending on the color of a person's skin or how much money he or she can afford to pay a legal "dream team."
- We can be angry about the perpetuation of a system that offers medical treatment, not on the basis of need, but on the basis of how much money someone has. The people who have no money and the people who have a lot of money get care — those in the middle may not.
- We can be angry about a society that allows a ready supply of deadly weapons to almost anyone with the result that, of all the technically advanced nations of the world, we have an exponentially higher murder rate than any other.
- We can be angry when women, though working every bit as hard as any man, still face discrimination, abuse, harassment, and unfair pay.
- We can be angry when white-collar criminals in corporate board rooms pay themselves fat salaries and bonuses, looting companies into bankruptcy, and leaving workers and retirees to fend for themselves.
- We can be angry at national priorities that allocate hundreds of billions of dollars to defense every year, equaling the amount allocated in total by all the other nations on the face

of the earth, almost 200 of them — when there are people right here in our own backyard who go without food, clothing, medicine because they need our help to get them.

Remember, God cares about justice.

Church Fights

No one in the church today knows what Euodia and Syntyche were fighting about. Must have been a battle royal for Paul to have heard of their spat, though. If it was the normal church knock-down, drag-out, it most likely dealt with incredibly important theological issues like the color of the new carpeting for the church sanctuary or whose recipe would appear first in the new women's association cookbook. Sad.

Obviously, these ladies are committed Christians because of the way they are described. Paul says that their "names are in the book of life." They are leaders in the church — Paul mentions how both labored, side by side together with him in spreading the gospel. The disagreement between the two was certainly of some consequence or Paul would not bring it to the attention of the whole church. Conflict involving the leadership of a church often causes the congregation to become polarized, and that could lead to who knows what kind of trouble.

Of course, some church conflict does indeed involve more serious issues than carpeting and cookbooks, and some of the uncivil behavior of the political arena has found its way under the steeple. The most recent evidence is the battle American mainstream churches have been having over the ordination of homosexuals. The Episcopal church has taken the most heat over the election of a man who happens to be homosexual as Bishop of New Hampshire. Some Episcopalians were thrilled; some were horrified. The rhetoric has been fast and furious, and, as is often the case, lots more heat than light was been generated. It is no exaggeration to say that this is now an ecclesiastical civil war.

As we say, the issue is not unique to Episcopalians. Most Protestant churches, including our own, are at varying stages of struggle with many questions about human sexuality. The pope has restated the Roman Catholic church's opposition to same-sex unions, but as the scandals of the past several years, largely of a homosexual nature show, the Catholic church has its own set of problems in this area.

Why is this such a huge topic of controversy in our churches? Simple. Because this is society's problem and we are a part of society. The problem is not going to just go away, whether the church wants it to or not. It would be wonderful if the church could speak with one voice on the issue, if Euodia and Syntyche could simply agree, but that is no more likely than Republicans and Democrats in Washington beginning to behave. And the issue is divisive enough as to threaten to tear churches apart the way our nation was torn before the War between the States.

Paul says this must stop. Do not dwell on the conflict, and his prescription lays out a plan:

- Rejoice in the Lord always. I will say it again: Rejoice!
- Let your gentleness be evident to all. The Lord is near.
- Do not be anxious about anything, but in everything, by prayer and petition, with thanksgiving, present your requests to God. And the peace of God, which transcends all understanding, will guard your hearts and your minds in Christ Jesus.

No question, there are wide divergences of social and theological views in the pews, but Paul would have us learn how to disagree without being disagreeable. Follow his advice: "Finally, brothers, whatever is true, whatever is noble, whatever is right, whatever is pure, whatever is lovely, whatever is admirable — if anything is excellent or praiseworthy — think about such things."

Proper 24
Pentecost 22
Ordinary Time 29
Matthew 22:15-22

One Nation, Under God

It is conventional wisdom that one must avoid talking about
religion or politics if we want to stay out of arguments. It is even
greater wisdom to keep religion and politics separate unless we are
ready to fight a firestorm. Think of the controversies about abortion, embryonic stem-cell research, and capital punishment as just
a few of the subjects bound to get folks choosing up sides.

Remember the mess not long ago when a federal appeals court
ruled that reciting the Pledge of Allegiance to the American flag in
public schools was unconstitutional because it contained the phrase,
"under God"? Members of the US House of Representatives as-
sembled on the steps of the Capitol to recite the Pledge in defiance.
The US Senate voted unanimously to condemn the decision. Across
the nation there appeared editorials, letters to the editor, and even
the occasional sermon decrying the action. The California man who
initiated the lawsuit was being cursed and vilified, threatened with
bodily harm and worse, by sweet church people who on Sunday
sing, "They'll know we are Christians by our love." Right! Over
and over there were complaints that these hallowed words, handed
down from generation to generation, were now being snatched from
our babies' mouths.

For what it is worth, those "hallowed words" have not been
around all that long. The pledge is only a little more than 100 years
old, written in 1892 for the celebration of the 400th anniversary of
Columbus' discovery of America.

For that matter, the phrase that has caused all the controversy
— "under God" — was not part of the original pledge anyway. It is

unclear precisely where the idea originated, but one driving force was the Catholic fraternal society, the Knights of Columbus. In the early '50s, the Knights themselves adopted the reworded pledge for use in their own meetings, and members bombarded Congress with calls for the United States to do the same. Other civic and fraternal organizations joined in. After all, the Cold War was raging and Joe McCarthy was finding godless communists under every rock — we were *not* godless, so in 1953, the change was formally proposed to Congress. It was approved the next year, and we who were in school at the time, had to relearn what we would repeat every morning.

As to the California case, the court held that it is an unconstitutional establishment of religion to require teachers to open every school day by leading students in a recitation of the Pledge, which includes the questionable phrase. Students do not have to repeat the words anyway. The US Supreme Court made that ruling long ago. No one can be forced to pledge allegiance to anything.

Keeping the sacred and secular separate has great precedent. The Pharisees and the Herodians, a strange partnership with only one thing in common — a big-time worry about the popularity of this new rabbi — come to Jesus and ask about the legitimacy of paying imperial taxes. It was a trap, as we all know, and as Jesus knew as well: force Jesus into a choice between alienating the crowds (who despised the heavy hand of Roman rule) or publicly proclaiming a treasonous point of view.

Jesus said, "Show me the coin used for paying the tax." They brought him a denarius, and he asked them, "Whose portrait is this? And whose inscription?"

"Caesar's," they replied.

Then he said to them, "Give to Caesar what is Caesar's, and to God what is God's."

Or to move that to the twenty-first century. "Give to the flag what is the flag's, and to God what is God's."

"One nation, under God ..." Good words. Perhaps unconstitutional words if we force someone to say them whose conscience is bothered by them. The freedom-loving nation to whom I pledge my allegiance would not do that. And neither would my God.

The God Of The Unlikely

Moses is one of the genuinely towering figures of the biblical story. Protected by God at his birth, chosen by God as a man, led by God throughout his career, buried by God at his death — as the scripture says, "Never since has there arisen a prophet in Israel like Moses ... unequaled for all the signs and wonders that the Lord sent him to perform ... for all the mighty deeds and all the terrifying displays of power ..." Hollywood needs a handsome, powerful Charleton Heston with flowing hair and full beard to begin to portray this "lion" of a man.

We find him here at the end of his life. Moses is on the mountaintop across the Jordan River from Jericho. Before him is a vast panorama. To the north is the Sea of Galilee, to the west is the Mediterranean, to the south is the vast Negev and the Jordan valley down to Zoar at the edge of the Dead Sea. For forty years he has led his people through one adventure after another to get to this place. Now he finally gets to see their new home, if only from a distance.

What was running through his mind at that moment, as he stared at the scene? As Moses looked back, it must have struck him how unlikely this all had been, and the only explanation could be that it was all in God's hands all along. Perhaps Yahweh might even be called "The God of the Unlikely":

- It was unlikely that he should have survived infancy, but God protected him ... the God of the unlikely.

- It was unlikely that a Hebrew child would be made a member of the Egyptian royal family, but God arranged it ... the God of the unlikely.
- It was unlikely that a prince would become a shepherd, learning what it took to care for an unruly flock (whether it be sheep or people), but God provided ... the God of the unlikely.
- It was unlikely that a tongue-tied, stammering eighty-year-old would inspire a nation of slaves or overwhelm a reluctant ruler, but God was behind it ... the God of the unlikely.
- It was unlikely that a people could survive as witless wilderness wanderers for forty years, but God protected ... the God of the unlikely.

As we move through scripture, the message is hammered home again and again. "Many who are first will be last, and the last will be first" (Matthew 19:30). Unlikely. "The greatest among you must become like the youngest, and the leader like one who serves" (Luke 22:26). Unlikely. The Savior of the world comes as a humble infant. Unlikely.

History is equally clear. Unlikely heroes arise. A poor boy raised in a log cabin and educated by the light of his fire becomes president and saves his nation from splintering. Lincoln. Unlikely. He was the inventor of the light bulb and the electrical system, which made it generally available, plus a practical telephone, the phonograph, the dictaphone, motion pictures, the storage battery, along with improvements in numerous other materials and processes, the holder of almost 1,100 patents. He only had three months of formal education before his teacher decided he was retarded and could not manage schooling. Thomas Edison. Unlikely. A black preacher's son who became a preacher himself changed the racial face of this nation — not a military leader or powerful politician, a preacher. Martin Luther King Jr. Unlikely.

It is interesting that just before his murder, Martin Luther King Jr. harked back to the story of Moses. It was the spring of 1968, and Dr. King was heavily involved with organizing what was known as the Poor People's Campaign, but in the midst of that he took time off to travel to Memphis, Tennessee, to lead a demonstration in support of higher wages for the garbage collectors of that city. At a rally on April 3, the day before he was gunned down on that motel balcony, he said,

> *I don't know what will happen now. We have got difficult days ahead. But it doesn't matter with me, because I've been to the mountaintop. Like anyone else, I want to live a long life. But I'm not concerned with that. I just want to do God's will and He has allowed me to go up the mountain. I see the promised land. I may not get there with you, but I want you to know tonight that we as a people will get to the promised land. I am happy tonight that I am not worried about anything. I'm not fearing any man. "Mine eyes have seen the glory of the coming of the Lord."*

No, Dr. King did not make it. He died outside the promised land of racial justice. He could see the land, but he never got there himself. It was the same with Moses. The Broadway or Hollywood ending to his life would have him marching triumphantly ahead of his grateful people as they enter Canaan, accompanied by a full-throated score played by soaring strings, crashing cymbals, and the rumble of drums. But no, for reasons that scripture never makes entirely clear, Moses would not cross over. After 120 years, Moses died there on the mountaintop, and was buried in some secret place known only to God. One more unlikely turn.

Moses, the liberator. Moses, the lawgiver. Moses, the leader. And as the scripture plainly acknowledges, Moses, "the servant of the Lord." But we would have to add unlikely in every case.

The message in all this is very simple: God chooses and God uses people and events that are often utterly beyond comprehension. Perhaps even me and you. We have all seen it, so be open to it, look forward to it, and even celebrate it. After all, you and I are servants of the God of the Unlikely.

169

The Truth

One of the first Bible verses my mother taught me when I was a little boy was "Lying lips are an abomination to the Lord," words that had a particular connection at that age to things like cookie jars. After I grew up, Mom and I were in conversation about some of the events in the news including the deception and prevarication that the stories often featured. I mentioned to her that some wag had said, "Lying lips may be an abomination to the Lord but sometimes they are a very present help in time of trouble."

Mom replied, "Who said that? Nobody you know!"

True. I do not know who said that, but I do know that truth is often a fragile commodity. But I also know who said, "You will know the truth, and the truth will set you free!" Jesus. What did he mean with those words? What truth? What freedom? After all, like beauty, truth and freedom are often in the eye of the beholder.

To be sure, Jesus gives us no clue as to which facts are definitive. And perhaps we have a handle on Jesus' meaning right there — facts often do not tell the story. It is possible for one to tell you all the facts and still not all the truth.

I recall a story of a ship's captain who entered the note into the logbook one day that the first mate was drunk. The mate later complained and asked that the remark be deleted. The captain replied, "It was the truth, wasn't it?"

"Well, yes, but ..."

"Then it stays!"

A few days later, with the captain in his bunk with a sudden fever, the mate had the responsibility of making entries in the log and wrote, "The captain is ill today with a high fever, but he is sober."

When the captain saw the entry, he exploded. "Why did you put such a thing in the log?"

The mate responded, "It was the truth, wasn't it?"

In the words of Oscar Wilde, "The pure and simple truth is rarely pure and never simple."

Perhaps this is where we get off the track. We try to take Jesus' words about the truth that makes for freedom and attach expository remarks — facts — to them. One pulpit explains Christian truth in terms of democratic ideals; another says Christian truth is found in personal piety; still another says Christian truth is learned in care for the disadvantaged. But Jesus did not do that. He did not define truth at all. In fact, in one of the most familiar New Testament verses, he says simply, "I AM ... the truth ..." (John 14:6).

To be honest, we would probably rather Jesus had given a definition, then our religion could be based on a convenient collection of do's and don'ts. We like the idea of a salvation we can get the old-fashioned way — earn it. But the word of the gospel is that freedom comes, not from *what* we know but *whom* we know. And if that were not the case, we would be much the poorer for it.

Family Resemblance

The internet is a fascinating place to hang out. Over the years there has been a wonderful accumulation of insightful material. For example, someone posted some interesting answers to science test questions as rendered by fifth and sixth graders. One youngster described the law of gravity as saying, "No fair jumping up without coming back down." Pretty good. Another said, "You can listen to thunder and tell how close you came to getting hit. If you don't hear it, you got hit, so never mind."

A couple of them responded to questions about clouds. One said, "I'm not sure how clouds are formed, but clouds know how to do it, and that's the important thing." Okay. Another said, "Water vapor gets together in a cloud. When it is big enough to be called a drop, it does." One defined a monsoon as a French gentleman.

A couple more. One youngster said, "When planets run around and around in circles, we say they are orbiting. When people do it, we say they are crazy." True. One defined the spinal column as "a long bunch of bones. The head sits on the top, and you sit on the bottom." Okay.

None of those have anything to do with the text, but this one jumped out at me because it surely does. One youngster wrote, "Genetics explains why you look like your father, and if you don't, why you should." In that context, this one really hits home: "How great is the love the Father has lavished on us, that we should be called children of God! And that is what we are!" Is there any family resemblance? There *should* be.

John Chrysostom, the great preacher of the middle ages, in his sermon on how to bring up children, advises parents to give their youngster some great scriptural name, to teach over and over the story of the original bearer of the name, and thus to give a standard to live up to, and an inspiration for living, when reaching adulthood. The epistle writer says we are in the family of God so we have the responsibility of doing the family proud and not besmirching the family name.

I love what follows: "Dear friends, now we are children of God, and what we will be has not yet been made known. But we know that when he appears, we shall be like him, for we shall see him as he is." God is not done with us yet. And amazingly, what lies in store is so wonderful it is beyond our comprehension.

Some years ago there was even a bomb threat at a meeting of the South Indiana Conference of the United Methodist Church. 1,800 United Methodists were gathered in an ordination service. Then a telephoned bomb threat came through. The auditorium at Indiana University quickly emptied.

The people left in a hasty and not-too-orderly fashion. Outside they discovered it was raining, but there was little complaining because they realized how much the rain was needed because of a drought. Forty-five minutes later, the crowd heard the announcement that the building has been searched and nothing was found. They could reenter.

As the wet Methodists started to enter through the door, security people kept repeating, "Please enter at your own risk!" Strange counsel for people entering a religious service. Or is it?

Imagine entering your church's narthex and your eyes falling upon a sign that reads, "Please enter at your own risk, because after the service, your life may never be the same again!"

"How great is the love the Father has lavished on us, that we should be called children of God! And that is what we are!" What a compliment that awaits you! You? A child of God? Oh, yes, I should have known. I can see the family resemblance.

Proper 26
Pentecost 24
Ordinary Time 31
Joshua 3:7-17

Memorial Day

The book of Joshua tells of Israel's conquest of Canaan, which appears to climax the long opening story of the Bible. In Genesis, God promises to give the land of Canaan to the descendants of Abraham, the people of Israel. Four hundred years of slavery in Egypt intervened. Then came Moses and delivery from bondage, but Israel wandered about in the wilderness long enough for an entire generation to die out and a new generation to take their place. Near the end of the book of Numbers, with Moses still in command, the Israelites conquer the promised land east of the Jordan River and finally arrive at their new home. The book of Deuteronomy consists of a long speech by Moses to the nation, including the last major installment of the law Moses passes on to Israel. At the end of Deuteronomy, Moses dies.

The book of Joshua continues the story from this point. First, God commissions Joshua and assures the people that he is indeed the chosen successor to Moses by the miraculous dry-land river crossing recounted in the text. Then, in an orgy of terror, violence, and mayhem, God takes the land of Canaan west of the Jordan away from its inhabitants and gives it to Israel under Joshua's command. Joshua, with the help of the priest Eleazar, distributes the conquered land to the tribes of Israel. Having aged, like Moses he bids his people farewell, dies, and is buried. Thus the book of Joshua explains how under Joshua's command Canaan was conquered, the Canaanites were slaughtered, and their lands were expropriated and redistributed to the tribes of Israel.

I wish the lectionary committee had not stopped so quickly with this text, because immediately following is a wonderful instruction to establish a memorial. "So Joshua called together the twelve men he had appointed from the Israelites, one from each tribe, and said to them, 'Go over before the ark of the Lord your God into the middle of the Jordan. Each of you is to take up a stone on his shoulder, according to the number of the tribes of the Israelites, to serve as a sign among you. In the future, when your children ask you, "What do these stones mean?" tell them that the flow of the Jordan was cut off before the ark of the covenant of the Lord. When it crossed the Jordan, the waters of the Jordan were cut off. These stones are to be a memorial to the people of Israel forever.' "

Remember *who* you are, *whose* you are, *where* you come from, and *where* you are going. Good advice to Israel, and good advice to all of us.

Proper 27
Pentecost 25
Ordinary Time 32
1 Thessalonians 4:13-18

Words Of Comfort

"Brothers [and sisters], we do not want you to be ignorant about those who fall asleep, or to grieve like the rest of men, who have no hope." The early church was anticipating the imminent return of the risen Christ. Indeed, some believers had even quit work, were waiting around idly for the glorious appearing, had exhausted their funds, and were now depending upon the generosity of the church to support them day to day. It grew to be such a frustration among that little-faith community that Paul would be prompted to write, "If a man will not work, he shall not eat" (2 Thessalonians 3:10). With the delay in Christ's return, life was keeping on keeping on, and, since death is a part of life, death was keeping on keeping on, too. It made grieving family and friends wonder what was to become of believers who have "fallen asleep." Are they going to miss out?

The first thing the apostle instructs is do not grieve as those "who have no hope." He does not say do not grieve. Grief is one of God's good gifts to help us deal with painful events. Anyone who has ever shed tears of sorrow knows what a wonderful catharsis a good cry can be. In fact, those who refuse to grieve appropriately can do themselves severe psychological damage.

In the congregation where I grew up, there was a wonderful lady who for years and years taught the kindergarten class in Sunday school. Her husband taught one of the adult classes; one of her daughters was our senior high leader. The husband died suddenly, a heart attack. Miss Emma refused to cry; she was convinced that weeping would not be a proper witness to her Christian faith. She

176

believed in life after death; she was confident that, one day, in the sweet by and by, there would be a wonderful reunion. So, no tears. That proved to be such a strain, that her mind snapped. She spent the last years of her life in a state hospital. So sad. No, Paul does not say do not grieve, but rather, do not grieve as those who have no hope.

What hope? Listen again: "We believe that Jesus died and rose again." That is the basis of our faith. Death — the event that elsewhere Paul called the final enemy — did not have the final word with Jesus. "... and so we believe that God will bring with Jesus those who have fallen asleep in him." Death did not have the final word with Jesus, nor us either. These friends who have died are not going to miss out on the glorious future that awaits.

The language that Paul uses to describe the day is magnificent. "For the Lord himself will come down from heaven, with a loud command, with the voice of the archangel and with the trumpet call of God, and the dead in Christ will rise first. After that, we who are still alive and are left will be caught up together with them in the clouds to meet the Lord in the air. And so we will be with the Lord forever." Glory! The sound of an enormous celestial reveille — as the old spiritual has it, "that great gittin' up morning."

Marvelous imagery. The trumpet was the traditional way to announce the arrival of a royal figure and the notion of "meeting the Lord in the air" speaks the language of power. This royal figure is not limited to particular territories; he is over all of them. Power!

Of course, the language is poetic, not photographic. This beautifully evocative passage has been misused in recent years by those so-called "prophecy-mongers." An unfortunate literalism about Paul's brief rhapsody depicting believers caught up in the clouds has become the basis for a lucrative industry about a "rapture," a relatively new phenomenon in the church and *not* traditional Christian teaching.

More than 400 years ago, in a time of even greater theological conflict about Christian teaching — the Reformation raging, people fighting and even dying in defense of their beliefs — two young men (one a pastor, the other a professor in the local university) were asked by their German governor to put on paper just what

Reformed Christians believed. They were asked to write in simple terms so the next generation, the youth, would not have all this trouble. The result of their work is called the "Heidelberg Catechism," a series of 129 questions and answers that provide an overview of the faith. They are all helpful, I suppose, but for me, the very first question and answer make the whole thing worthwhile: "What is your only comfort in life and in death?" The answer:

> *That I belong — body and soul, in life and in death — not to myself, but to my faithful Savior Jesus Christ who, at the cost of his own blood has fully paid for all my sins ... that he protects me so well that, without the will of my Father in heaven, not a hair can fall from my head; indeed, that everything must fit his purpose for my salvation. Therefore, by his Holy Spirit he assures me of eternal life, and makes me wholeheartedly willing and ready from now on to live for him.*

My only comfort — I belong to Jesus, and nothing can ever change that ... not even death. Therefore, "encourage each other with these words."

Proper 28
Pentecost 26
Ordinary Time 33
Matthew 25:14-30

Talents

Three servants. One received five talents with which to trade (by the way, talents were significant amounts of money — the equivalent of fifteen years' wages for a laborer). The first fellow followed the market closely, knew the prospects of the crops, anticipated the arrival of the caravans from Damascus, and marked the movement of the Roman legions. On the information he gleaned, he invested his five talents shrewdly — he made a profit of 100% on his transactions. Not bad.

Another servant was entrusted with two talents. Here was a blunt and honest man, probably a down-to-earth fellow who believed in getting money the old-fashioned way: earn it. I can envision him as a farmer, driving his oxen hard, tending his vineyards carefully, and laboring from sunup to sundown. By the sheer faithfulness of day-to-day work, he made his two talents yield another two — a total of four.

The third servant was different. He hid his one talent in the ground. The action, as judged by the standards of that day, was not lazy. To hide money in the ground was the traditional way of saving. He was scrupulous with what he had been given — too scrupulous. That was his downfall. He would have been a better servant had he planned and risked and lost.

It is hard to escape the conviction that the story was told mainly for the one-talent fellow's benefit. There are far more one-talent men and women in this world than five-talent people. Only a very few have the literary capabilities of a Shakespeare or a Hemingway; only a few have the inventive abilities of a Thomas Edison; only a few have the musical abilities of a Bach or a Beethoven or even the Beatles; only a few can preach like Billy Graham. The temptation for the one-talent person is to say, "I don't have much, so don't expect anything of me. What can I do?" But the real reason for the one-talent fellow's failure (and in Jesus' mind, the big danger that faces *all* one-talent people) is fear — the man said, "I did not use what I was given because I was afraid." He had paralysis from analysis.

This story has given an important word to our language — talents. No longer do we think of a talent as a sum of money, but rather an ability or collection of abilities that allow individuals to excel. Any assumption that "all men (or all women) are created equal" (despite what the Declaration of Independence might say) or any demand for such equality is foolishness. Jesus knew and clearly taught that people differ in talents.

What is your *talent*? It should be noted that the story does not indicate that anyone received no talent. No one was left empty-handed. Everyone is in some regard "talented," and remember, the talent is no small sum. Don't lose it! Use it!

Edward Everett Hale once said, "I am only one, but I am one. I cannot do everything, but I can do something. I will not let what I cannot do interfere with what I can do."

The Incredible Invitation

Imagine for a moment. You go out to your mailbox tomorrow and begin to sift through the contents: some bills, some junk mail, and so on. But your eye lights on one particular envelope that strikes your attention. The return address is simply, The White House, Washington DC. You look at it and wonder to yourself, "What in the world could it be?" You don't wait to get back to the house to find out about this one. You open the envelope and find inside an engraved invitation: "The President and Mrs. Astafickjickle cordially invite you to a state dinner in honor of the Prime Minister of Botswanaland at 8 p.m., January 30, 2009. Black Tie. RSVP." Wow! An invitation to the White House.

What will you do? It's not cheap to travel to Washington DC. The airfare is pricey. And then there's the hotel room and cabs and other meals, not to mention the souvenirs that you will have to bring back for family and friends. We are beginning to talk some serious money here. So what do you do? Do you accept the invitation in spite of the cost, or do you just toss it in the trash and not give it a second thought? Ha! You know very well that you would probably move heaven and earth for the chance to do something like that.

Suppose you have a good friend who is close to one of your favorite entertainers, a big name on a level with the late Frank Sinatra, for example. Suddenly, this friend invites you to come to Atlanta where the concert tour is stopping and spend the day with this big star, to be a part of the entourage, to get to sit and talk and just relax with one of the biggest names in show business. Would you go? You bet your life. After all, how many times in a lifetime do chances like this come along?

Suppose another situation: Out of the blue, literally, you get an invitation to visit with ... Jesus. Of course, this visit will not be in the White House or in a fancy hotel suite. But for someone who claims to be one of Jesus' followers, a Christian, that really shouldn't matter. But this is a different kind of invitation — it's not for dinner. Unless you bring the food. It's not even necessarily in a home — it might be in a sharecropper's shack; it might even be in a jail. It is certainly not "dress-up," because your host has nothing to "dress-up" with. Strange invitation, isn't it? Would you go?

Okay, enough with the imagining. We can fantasize about an invitation for dinner at the White House; we can dream about being able to spend leisurely hours with big stars. But that last one, the one inviting us to be with Jesus, is no fantasy. That one is real. And we read the invitation in the text.

"Whatever you did for one of the least of these brothers of mine, you did for me." That man is unable to get work because all he knows is mill work and he can't get a job because of the problems in the textile industry, Jesus is saying *he* is that man. Or the little old woman who, after almost ninety years of life, is now desperately lonely because she can't get out of the house, Jesus is saying the *he* is that woman. Or the young teenager who got hooked on drugs while trying to keep up with the fast life of his buddies, now in jail, caught for thievery to support his habit, Jesus is saying *he* is that boy. Or the little girl down in Central America, not knowing where or when she will get her next meal and not having any idea why her life should be that way, Jesus is saying *he* is that little girl. An invitation for us to come by. An invitation for us to take seriously. "Whatever you did for one of the least of these brothers of mine, you did for me."

Leaping Lepers

Leaping lepers. That is as good an image as any for the sight of a rag-tag bunch hustling down the road to the temple. Scripture was clear: "The person with such an infectious disease must wear torn clothes, let his hair be unkempt, cover the lower part of his face and cry out, 'Unclean! Unclean!' As long as he has the infection he remains unclean. He must live alone; he must live outside the camp" (Leviticus 13:45-46).

Leprosy. What we now know as Hansen's Disease, which destroys the nerves in the fingers and toes making them insensitive to pain and finally leads the victims to wear their limbs down through repeated injuries, but also any one of a number of other skin diseases. Unclean. The Hebrew people had a thing about skin diseases. Even sacrificial animals — goats or sheep or doves — that happened to have a mottled or blemished coat were routinely rejected from the temple rituals (good thing for the animals, I guess — it saved them from the slaughter!). But human beings whose body's outer "coat," as it were, happened to be blotched or mottled or visibly birthmarked were often equally rejected. Their condition was seen as a mark of divine judgment. They were shunted off to the fringes, out of sight, if not out of mind. They were encouraged, when they did draw close to an inhabited town, to cover their faces with hoods and veils. Some of this was because their diseases were thought to be highly contagious — although, truth be told, it was just as much because they simply looked different. No wonder that lepers tended to travel in packs — it was for their own protection. It was a miserable life.

Then came Jesus. By this point, his fame had begun to spread. After all, word of someone who can routinely do the miraculous things that Jesus did was bound to get around. Three days before, Jesus had healed a leper. Whether these ten had heard about that and were thinking that this might be their lucky day is a matter of conjecture, but from the appropriate distance, they cry out, "Jesus, Master, have pity on us!" Perhaps they were just looking for a hand-out. Who knows? "Jesus, Master, have pity on us!"

And he did. But not in the way we might have expected. He did not go over to these sad sufferers, did not lay hands on them or offer a kind blessing. He just yelled back — "Go, show yourselves to the priests." Standard operating procedure according to the book of Leviticus (14:1-32). Once you have been declared ritually unclean on account of a skin disease, the only road back to polite society — in the unlikely event of a healing — is to go to a priest. He will examine your skin, then put you through a ritual of religious purification, and voilá, you are back again. So, all ten lepers, simply on Jesus' say-so, head off down the road, in search of a priest. No indication of any hesitancy on their part. Off they go ... even before they are healed. Amazing. As we know, their step of faith was certainly rewarded. As Luke recounts it, "as they went, they were cleansed." Now we have those Leaping Lepers!

Hallelujah! Head 'em up, move 'em out. Off they ran as fast as they could go to see a husband, a wife, a son or daughter, a father or mother, a grandfather or grandmother they had not seen for who knows how long. Off they ran to see their fields, their fishing boat, their friends. As fast as they could go. No longer yelling "unclean," now clean! Ten lepers leaping, and a partridge in a pear tree.

But wait, one of them is coming back and he is yelling something. What's that? As the text says, he was "praising God in a loud voice." He comes right up to Jesus, throws himself at the Master's feet ... and says, "Thank you." Nice touch. And ever since, the other nine have been beaten up by preachers through the centuries as incredible, ungrateful wretches.

Is that the point of all this? If it is, I want to offer a word or two in defense of the nine. First off, they did exactly what Jesus told them to do. There is no indication of any reluctance on their part.

There is certainly no indication of ingratitude. Jesus says "Go," so they go. Sounds like obedient faith to me.

The point of part one of the story is that there is *nothing* beyond the power of God. Even something as awful as leprosy (or AIDS or cancer or heart disease; insert what you will in there). And note that there was no question asked of these ten about their faith in advance of the miracle. Forget any quid pro quo's like "If you have enough faith, this or that will happen." Nope. Jesus just did it. Almost by long distance even. "Go, show yourselves to the priests."

Then we come to part two. "One of them, when he saw he was healed, came back, praising God in a loud voice. He threw himself at Jesus' feet and thanked him — and he was a Samaritan." A Democrat. A Republican. Insert what you will. Good guy, regardless.

Yes, this story has been used for generations at this time of the year. Thanksgiving, the time to count your blessings, name them one by one, and thank God, just like our good guy hero. But the story continues. Jesus asked, "Were not all ten cleansed? Where are the other nine? Was no one found to return and give praise to God except this foreigner?"

Despite the fact that this text has been used for years as a club to beat us into being more thankful (as if that were really possible anyway), this is not, fundamentally, a story about giving thanks. Rather, it is about seeing something. When Jesus chides the other nine for not returning, it is not because he feels personally slighted. It is because only this man — this unbeliever, according to conventional wisdom — has realized that his healing is an act of God. Jesus does not say of the nine, "Was none of them found to return and say thank you except this foreigner?" No, what he actually says is, "Was no one found to return and give praise to God...?"

To be honest, if there is anything for which to give thanks this week, this may be the most important. Being able to see what is right in front of us all the time. Origen of Alexandria once remarked that holiness is seeing with the eyes of Christ. Thomas Aquinas said that the ultimate goal of the Christian life is a "beatific vision," an act of seeing. The Samaritan saw something, and it changed his life. Not only was he healed, he was made whole.

WARNING
Removing or tampering with the card on the back side of this page renders this book non-returnable.

Title: Lectionary Tales For The Pulpit, Series V,
Cycle A

ISBN: 0-7880-2454-X

INSTRUCTIONS TO ACCESS PASSWORD FOR ELECTRONIC COPY OF THIS TITLE:

The password appears on the reverse side of this page. Carefully cut the card from the page to retrieve the password.

Once you have the password, go to

http:/www.csspub.com/passwords/

and locate this title on that web page. By clicking on the title, you will be guided to a page to enter your password, name, and email address. From there you will be sent to a page to download your electronic version of this book.

For further information, or if you don't have access to the internet, please contact CSS Publishing Company at 1-800-241-4056 in the United States (or 419-227-1818 from outside the United States) between 8 a.m. and 5 p.m., Eastern Standard Time, Monday through Friday.